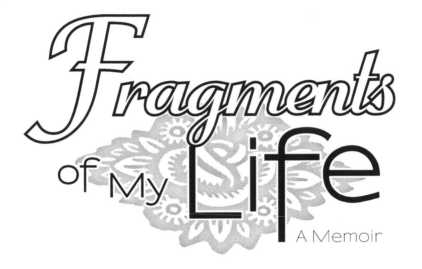

Fragments of My Life

A Memoir

Rita Braun

iUniverse, Inc.
Bloomington

Fragments of My Life
A Memoir

Copyright © 2013 Eduardo Karpat

iUniverse books may be ordered through booksellers or by contacting:

iUniverse
1663 Liberty Drive
Bloomington, IN 47403
www.iuniverse.com
1-800-Authors (1-800-288-4677)

Cover design by Georgina Duarte -
georduartes@gmail.com - of www.amandinajoyeria.com

ISBN: 978-1-4759-6696-1 (sc)
ISBN: 978-1-4759-6697-8 (hc)
ISBN: 978-1-4759-6698-5 (e)

Library of Congress Control Number: 2012923764

Printed in the United States of America

iUniverse rev. date: 5/17/2013

Rita Braun

Fragments of a Life, A Memoir

1st Edition—April 2008 (São Paulo, Brazil)
2nd Edition—September 2010 (São Paulo, Brazil)

Rita Braun

Translated into English from the original Portuguese by Giles Beard and Mark Philipps, Talking Business, São Paulo. www.talkingbusiness.com.br

This photo was torn from a wall and damaged by a soldier's boot, deforming the nose. Our maid saw it and kept the photo until the end of the war so she could return it to us. Thanks to the work of a painter, it has been restored.

This book is dedicated to the memory of my mother, Mina Maria Ringel, who was a role model for me and for all who knew her.

I have learned that a life is worth nothing,
but also that nothing is worth a life.
—André Malraux

We are made of flesh, but must live as if we were steel.
—Sigmund Freud

Contents

Foreword

In these *Fragments of a Life*, Rita Braun records various aspects of the life of a "woman of valor" (from the Hebrew *eshet chayil*).

It falls to us to understand how to take positives from the suffering of the past, while always maintaining a critical detachment and not getting lost in sentiments of hate and revenge. On the contrary, let us learn to live with the past and the uncountable moments of deep suffering.

Since I first had the immense pleasure of meeting Rita in 1996, through a project to interview survivors of the Holocaust here in Brazil, for the USC Shoah Foundation Institute of Los Angeles—an organization created by Steven Spielberg—I can say that we have become increasingly close. I have been able to sense in her an educational mission to create a better future for this world.

She showed, and shows, courage and a great sense of self-esteem in not expressing any feelings of guilt for having survived, which can sometimes happen with survivors. Despite her own suffering, she, together with her mother, helped to hide others at a time when they lived a clandestine life under a false identity.

Rita has become a true working companion of mine, always willing to talk to youngsters in schools, to guide university students in their work on the subject, or to answer the call whenever people have requested the presence or words of a Holocaust survivor who expresses herself calmly and lucidly.

In coordinating a work that has resulted in the production

of an educational documentary, we have had the pleasure to include Rita as one of the contributors. The strength and clarity with which she expresses herself give veracity to her accounts.

These "fragments" record happy and sad moments of her life. The words and pages flow, inviting us to reflect on our own lives and, at times, even to rethink certain concepts.

Anita Pinkuss
Coordinator of the Remembrance Project
at the Jewish Cultural Centre Representative
of the Shoah Foundation SP

Acknowledgments

All my love to my husband, Mauricio; my children, Eliana and Edmundo; my daughter-in-law, Lilian; and my grandchildren, Claudia, Eduardo, and Allan.

Without their encouragement and support, I would not have faced this challenge.

If Only I Were …

There were wires in the ghetto
On the wall so high,
And there through a crack
Suddenly appeared a cat.

The feline stretched
And with a deep yawn,
Crossed the wall of the ghetto
To the other side of the world.

The sentry saw the cat,
For the gate looked on nearby,
But didn't hear the scream
Or the gunfire or grenade.

The pussycat reached the alley
In search of the mouse.
O merciful God,
Why didn't you make me a cat?

Rita Braun, 1992

Katowice Kraków

Map of Poland
Katowice
Kraków
The cities Stanislavov, Stryi, and Boryslav were ceded to Ukraine,
and they were returned to Poland long after the war.

Introduction

Fragments of a Life
A Memoir

Today is the first of May 1991, the day on which my granddaughter Claudia (or "Claudinha" as we call her) completes fourteen years. How quickly the time flies! It seems like yesterday.

I remember Mother preparing the bag for the extended holiday in Guarujá when suddenly there was a phone call. It was my daughter, Eliana, announcing that she was on the road to motherhood.

When Mother heard the news, she immediately unpacked the bags and came with us to await the arrival of the first granddaughter and great-granddaughter. Granddaughter and great-granddaughter ... yes, since we were both sure that it would be a girl.

On opening an old notebook, I found these notes that I wrote following this extra-special event I was able to share with my mother, two years before her death. When I think about this, I still feel moved, knowing that this period was, without any doubt at all, the happiest of her life.

If the birth of a child is a moment of extreme happiness for a mother, the birth of a grandchild or great-grandchild is sublime, magical.

Three years later, when I received the news that my grandson Eduardo had been born, I felt so anxious and emotional on the way to the maternity ward that I drove

1

into a supermarket cart that a gentleman was pushing. When I apologized and asked if he was hurt, he shouted, "Hurt? You almost killed me, lady!"

With the arrival of my youngest grandson, Allan, I was an old hand. Even so, the emotion of seeing the tiny defenseless being exiting his mother's womb was extraordinary! It was the first time that I had watched a childbirth through the window of an operating theater.

Many images flashed through my mind like scenes from a movie, now flashing up randomly, now in sequence. It was the beginning of a new life, of a new hope that would certainly bring a lot of happiness.

I mention all this to explain why I have finally resolved to answer the insistent requests from my children and grandchildren, made over many years, to write my life story.

The most recent and forceful of these requests came from my grandson Eduardo, who had been hounding me over this for many months. I also received an e-mail from my granddaughter Claudia, who is studying in Paris, following up her request that I write, and saying that my story would be the biggest gift that I could give my children, grandchildren, great-grandchildren, and—using her words—everyone who had the opportunity to read it. Given this, I committed myself to writing at least a page per day, in order to complete this mission on time.

Before that, I had actually never had any intention of publishing a book. I wish only to leave a record for my descendants, the most vivid memories from my childhood and adolescence, and to tell them about their ancestors. Unfortunately, they have (except the younger ones) met only two of them: my mother and her brother, my uncle Filip.

Miriam, Uncle Filip's daughter and her husband, Jacob.
Below: Uncle Filip and Mother.

For this reason, at first sight, some details may seem very personal, but actually they reveal how the life of a happy girl, full of dreams and plans for the future, was abruptly ruined, transforming paradise on earth into an indescribable hell.

Rather than making an untimely leap straight into the horrors of the Holocaust, in which more than six million unarmed and defenseless human beings were eliminated in the most brutal and cold-blooded fashion, I have preferred to start by talking about my life before the five years of terror that I lived through ... and which live with me even today, in my memories.

I hope that this account, in addition to being a gesture of love to my family, represents a warning to future generations about how intolerance can lead to a process of total dehumanization.

During the war, when the trucks carrying the Jews to the concentration camps passed along the streets of the ghetto[1] in the direction of the exit, it was common to hear the screams of the prisoners pleading, "Whoever survives must tell everyone what happened to us!".

Without yet knowing that I would be one of the survivors, I subconsciously took on this commitment, and to this day I dedicate myself to communicating the cruelties to which we were subjected. I hope that this book helps ensure that the circumstances that led to the Holocaust never arise again.

---

1   Ghetto: district surrounded by walls and electric fences in which Jews were confined during the Second World War.

The Girl Within Me

Going back in time, I'll begin by describing the most relevant facts, from my birth until today. All of the events described herein are real, as are the names of the people involved and the cities mentioned. Some passages may seem overly sentimental in the eyes of the reader, but they were all very important to me.

Everything that I have experienced, and the good and bad memories associated with these events, has gone into making me who I am, shaping my personality. But the most important thing is that the atrocities I have lived through haven't managed to diminish my enthusiasm, the value I place on life, and my desire to live each moment to the fullest.

I recognize that there are good and bad qualities in everyone, and for this reason I accept and like people as they are. Moreover, I still sense that within me lives a young girl, who keeps me happy-go-lucky, as they say, despite the maturity and limitations that age brings.

I think that if this girl ever disappears, in a way it will mean the end of my hopes and dreams and plans. Ultimately, I think it is thanks to her that I have managed to transform ashes and bitterness into examples of life that, I hope, make the world a better place.

Mother, before the war.

Father.

Part One:
Before The War

How It All Began

My father's name was Maurycy David Hitner, and his nickname was Edmund. My mother was called Mina and was nicknamed Nusia.

After a seven-year engagement, my mother and father married and went to live in the city of Kraków (former capital of Poland). It was there that I was born, on May 28, 1930, weighing ten pounds.

I was given the name Henrieta Roza Hitner, but I have dropped the name Roza and added a *t* to Henrieta, becoming Henrietta. They nicknamed me Rita because, according to Mother, the name Henrieta was very long and formal for such a small girl. They cut Henrieta in half, and it became Rita forever. I liked it!

Some days before I was born, my mother's bedroom was sterilized, along with all the bedclothes, towels, and instruments needed to conduct the birth.

Afraid that newborn children could be mixed up in the maternity ward, Mother decided to have the child at home. Professor-Doctor Szymanowicz, a famous surgeon of that time, was hired along with his team. The birth took three days.

The amount of disappointment I caused by being born a girl was enormous, as Mother feared she would have to have as many children as necessary to produce a male heir, and thus preserve the Hitner surname, a name my father carried as the only son of an important Jewish-Polish aristocratic family.

My mother's first reaction on seeing me was, "It wasn't worth all that suffering to produce a girl!" But her disappointment didn't in any way diminish the immense love she felt for me, despite the severity with which she raised me.

During the war, however, she thanked God for having had a girl, as it would have been impossible to hide a circumcised boy.

Some weeks after I was born, our family moved to the city of Katowice, where my maternal grandparents lived, Berta and Salo Blum.

Me, at six months.

My Father's Family

Unfortunately, I never got to know my paternal grandparents, who died before I was born. Everything that I know of them was told to me by my father.

Grandfather Oscar was a local patriarch, owner of the Sosnica farm, where he organized traditional festivals at the end of each harvest. The farmworkers brought their offerings in enormous baskets carried on their shoulders. On receiving this tribute, Grandfather invited the cutest of the farmworkers to open the festival by dancing with him.

He died at age forty-two, following a hunt. After pursuing a hart at a gallop, he drank a little cool water from a creek and lay down on the grass still sweating. Thus he contracted pneumonia, from which he died.

His funeral was very grand, with the whole city of Przemysl turning out. Authorities, representatives of the Catholic Church and of the Jewish community, were there in large numbers, in recognition and mourning. The funeral cortege stretched along the main street of the city. The coffin was carried in a glass carriage, and alongside a page led his horse, which neighed and pranced continually, rearing up in grief at the loss of his owner. His tomb was completely covered by the flowers of well-wishers.

All this honor was bestowed on my grandfather because he had been an illustrious benefactor to the city: in winter he sent large quantities of wood to heat the churches and synagogues, as well as food and money for the less well-off.

My grandmother Helena died of a massive heart attack at the age of forty-five, while taking afternoon tea.

Thus my father became an orphan at the age of seventeen. An only child, young and wealthy, he didn't have the experience to manage the land inherited from his father. So he sold it and went into cinematography, representing Warner Brothers for the whole of Poland. Later, after marrying my mother, he bought a cinema in Kraków.

My Mother's Family

My grandmother Berta Blum.

My grandfather Salo Blum.

My mother's family comprised grandparents Salo and Berta Blum, my aunt Ala, and my uncles, Edmund, Filip, and Edward. My grandfather Salo was a businessman, owner of a chain of shoe stores, Blum & Binder, in Katowice.

Binder was the name of the firm's junior partner. They manufactured, and also imported, the latest styles of footwear from Vienna and Prague. I remember that when there was a fight between the partners, Mother was called on as a peacemaker. Mr. Binder used to say that Mother was "the lady lawyer of the family," since she always resolved conflicts between the partners in a diplomatic fashion.

Grandpa Salo was a very elegant and vain man. The tailor who made his suits copied his designs from the American movie star Gary Cooper. In order to get everything just so, Grandpa paid for the tailor to go to the cinema so that he could see the suit he had to copy.

Grandpa traveled abroad frequently, in order to attend expositions and bring back the latest fashions for his stores.

He was a much respected businessman, whose word was worth any signature.

Grandma Berta was a witty, vivacious, elegant lady, whose hats were specially ordered from the milliner and delivered directly to her home. Her activities at home consisted of managing the domestic staff, planning the menu for the week, and allocating the funds needed to buy the provisions.

At the Krynica spa: Mother with her parents and youngest brother, Edward.

Auntie Ala.

In addition, she led an intense social life, frequenting the tearooms, where she met up with her friends and daughters (she always enjoyed the company of those younger than herself) and hosting musical gatherings and fund-raising card-playing afternoons.

I went with my grandma to concerts, theatrical productions, and shows of all types, and we also participated in various fund-raising events for both the community and outside.

My grandparents used to spend their vacations at spas such as Carlsbad or Krynica, where they met the elite of Polish society.

Aunt Ala, who was one year younger than Mother and extremely vain, was a very eccentric character in both her manner and dress sense. Separated from her husband, Dolek, she didn't have any children, but she took great care of her fox terrier, the little dog Tchiky.

She always dressed elegantly and originally, but in a way that was sure to attract attention. I especially remember one of her hats, which was decorated with a little chimney that had some tulle rising up like smoke.

The heels of her shoes matched the color of her bag or scarf. As she didn't like her front teeth and wanted to have a perfect smile, she didn't think twice about ordering caps, which were rare at that time.

What fascinated me about her was the way her wavy hair framed her face. As she moved her head, the curls twisted in artistic disarray. And the many bracelets she wore jangled with a tinkle I found delightful.

She never used to pay me a lot of attention, as she was always busy with her many commitments. The way she used to show her affection was in giving presents. It was she who gave me my first fur coat with a bonnet and *mufka* (muff).

Aunt Ala was jealous of my mother, even though both of them were very beautiful in their different ways. Mother dressed in a classical, elegant style, while my aunt was more flamboyant.

Uncle Edmund, who was the eldest of the sons and had the same name as my father, was a lawyer of renown and uncommon intellect. Everybody rightly considered him a "walking encyclopedia." He spoke seven languages fluently and was a respected philatelist, in addition to playing the piano by ear.

Edmund Blum.

It was enough for me to sing a new melody, which I would present while dancing, and Uncle Edmund would immediately accompany me on the piano. He was very charming and was always surrounded by beautiful women. My love for him became idolization. He was my hero and I his acolyte.

Mother's brothers: Uncles Filip and Edmund, with Kora.

Thanks to him, I got into junior high school without difficulty, after not having studied for the five years that the war lasted. But I'm getting ahead of myself ...

My mother's second brother, Filip (who, coincidentally, shared a name with the man who would become her second husband), was a year younger than Edmund and was another heartthrob. He graduated in advertising, was well respected and handsome, and possessed an irresistible charm. He boasted two dimples, and his smile was contagious. The prosperity of his company allowed him to realize a dream trip to Brazil in 1939 and thus escape the atrocities of the Nazis.

The physical appearance of the two brothers was disarming, albeit in different ways. Edmund was slighter, with a lordly bearing and a diplomatic manner, and he dressed accordingly. Filip had a stronger physique, with broad shoulders, and he had a roguish, charming smile.

At mealtimes, my place was, tiresomely, next to Uncle Filip, who wouldn't let me put my elbows on the table, or swing my legs, or eat with my elbows out. And to remind me to keep my elbows next to my body, he would sometimes make me eat with a book under each arm.

Finally, there was the youngest brother, Edward; born during the First World War, he had a difficult temperament, typical (they said) of a "child of war." He was handsome but serious. Of the five siblings, only Mother and he had blue eyes. He was jealous of me because, when I was born, he lost the status of being the "baby" of the family. He was noble and very loyal. Being the youngest child, some ten years younger than his brother Filip, he kept himself—or was kept—apart. A student of dentistry, before he graduated even, he used to work at home filling the teeth of his companions by using the motor from a sewing machine. Very modest with regard to his achievements, he never mentioned that he had dated Kora, the daughter of my future stepfather.

The great affinity between Mother and Uncle Filip led to a strong bond between them. Aunt Ala and Uncle Edmund were another pair who were very close. My grandmother had a preference for Edmund, and Grandpa for my mother.

In truth, they were all adored and blessed with the love, affection, and respect of their parents. As with all families, there were disagreements, such as when Uncle Filip felt hurt by his mother's attitude after he asked her to keep safe a tidy sum of money that he had accumulated. Heeding the tugs at a mother's heartstrings, when Uncle Edmund needed money, Grandma Berta didn't think twice about passing on the savings of the one brother to the other. Despite this, Uncle Filip didn't hold a grudge.

From left to right: Edward, Kora, Ala, and my father, Edmund.
Edward on the farm, during a hunt.

A break during a hunt, uncle Edward.

Seated: Mother, two cousins, and Uncle Edward. Standing:
Uncle Edmund, cousin Lundek, and Uncle Filip.

Above all, the atmosphere that reigned in my grandparents' house was always one of joy, harmony, and unity. I remember that when my grandmother fell sick and needed to go to the hospital, Uncle Filip—the strongest of the three brothers—took her in his arms and carried her to the ambulance all the way down from the second floor.

My grandparents' house was called "the doll's house," since both the daughters and the sons were very handsome. The local families in the community sighed at the prospect of my uncles—Edmund, Filip, and Edward—pairing off with their daughters. All the same, none of them married. I think they were very demanding and at the same time content with living in their parents' house. Although the daughters married, they were not happy marriages: both of them divorced.

Innocent Pursuits

I soon perceived that life could be very interesting, even as the only child in the house and having nothing to do, as I loved to follow adult conversations unnoticed.

To do this, I found the perfect place. I used to stay hidden beneath the enormous dining table, which was covered by a large embroidered green velvet cloth that had long fringes reaching down to the floor.

Happy in childhood.

From here I was able to hear any conversation I chose, without anyone knowing I was there. I had a lot of fun under there. Some people took off a shoe, probably to relieve a discomfort, or shifted their legs. Others exercised their toes.

The adults were generally so self-absorbed that they didn't notice when I sneaked out of my hiding place the minute that the topic of conversation turned less interesting. I then went to play with my dolls or to do my homework, but I returned immediately when the conversation dropped to a whisper.

My favorite pastime was walking. Nearly every afternoon, I went out on my beautiful silent blue metal *hulajnoga* (kick scooter), with its rubber wheels and loud bell. I mention these details because, in those days, kick scooters were generally made from wood and didn't have springs, which made them noisy.

I used to go to the park, but not before going to the bakery, where for fifty *groszy* (cents), I could buy a sweetbread filled with cheese that I used to savor.

On other occasions, I'd go to the cinema for free, as my father was known among the cinematographic circles, and watch the cartoons that they used to show ahead of the movie.

Playing with my little dog Tchiky.

It was enough for me to present myself at the ticket office as Edmund Hitner's daughter for them to let me in. After the cartoons finished, I was asked to leave the auditorium, as usually the movies were prohibited to minors. Thus I was a happy child, who always gladly welcomed the gifts life handed my way, however small they were.

My Parents' Separation

At eight years old, on a day trip.

A trip to the park with Uncle Filip. Looking at the fish.

In 1938, to my great sadness, my parents divorced. Father moved to Warsaw, while Mother and I went to live with my maternal grandparents in Katowice.

In truth, their separation had been coming for a while.

When I realized that Father was almost never at home, I asked my mother why. She told me that he needed to be in Warsaw because of his work, but he would always visit me whenever his professional commitments allowed.

After the separation, Mother was invited to supervise the cinemas in Katowice and other cities nearby; she accepted with pleasure, because she always liked to keep herself busy.

As her work required continual travel, albeit very short trips, I was placed in the care of my grandparents, which included sleeping in their bedroom.

All the same, my childhood was so wonderful that my parents' separation had almost no effect on my happiness.

Of course on trips, which were always made with one rather than both of them, it made me sad to see other children playing with both their parents. But my parents made sure that they were always present in my life, even while they were separated.

Improvised Conductor

Greatly loved by my grandparents, aunt, and uncles, although not a spoiled child, I was fought over by everyone on Sundays, to be taken on trips or other amusements, such as going skating or to the cinema, theater, circus, or snack bar.

I remember that one Sunday morning, my grandfather took me to a candy store with live music. We were enjoying a delicious ice cream when suddenly the children present were invited by the bandleader to go onstage and show off their "talent."

Some recited poetry; others sang accompanied by the orchestra. I recall a girl who won a bar of chocolate for reciting a verse. Next, a boy stood on a chair to reach the microphone and sang a song, winning a box of lollipops.

I didn't want to take part because, to my surprise and horror, I couldn't remember anything. But my grandfather literally dragged me onto the stage and put me up on the chair next to the bandleader, asking him to introduce me. I stood there desperately trying to think of something, so as not to disappoint my grandfather, who had returned to the table, eyes shining, ready to burst into applause.

The people sat around the room were watching me, waiting for something that simply wasn't happening. I could dance (which I found easy, even improvising), but there was no space to do so.

Then out of the blue, I had a brilliant idea: I asked for the leader's baton and said that I would conduct the orchestra. They started to play ... and it worked! By pure luck, knowing the melody, I was able to keep the rhythm well, to the complete jubilation of my grandfather. And this was how I made my "triumphant entry" into artistic life.

As a prize, I won a box of champagne cookies, just the sort of cookie that I never liked and still don't like even today.

Other Activities

From the time I was three years old, Mother took me to rhythmic gymnastics classes, which, according to her, I enjoyed a lot. Over time, I moved on to ballet and piano lessons, which also gave me a lot of pleasure.

At school, I loved to take part in every type of cultural event. I remember, one Mother's Day, paying tribute to my mother by reciting the following verse:

Mamusiu moja droga
Co dzien prosze Boga
By zdrowie i sily
Zawsze Ci sluzyly.

My dearest Momma, each day
I look to God and pray
That health and energy
Will always keep you company.

I saw my mother smiling at me from among all of the mothers. I waved to her happily. When a friend asked me which one was my mother, I answered without missing a beat, "The one in the middle, the most beautiful one."

I attended a public school in the city of Katowice. Early in the morning, I would drink just a little cup of cream from the boiled milk, but in my lunch box I would pack a delicious egg sandwich, which is still my favorite sandwich today.

In winter, the servants helped me to dress, tying my shoelaces. When my school bag, which I carried on my back, got too heavy, one of them would help me with it.

When I enrolled at school, I was given a beautiful crocodile bag that had a gorgeous smell of leather. It's strange how certain aromas are stored in our memories—I still remember this smell even today.

The Vacation that Changed My Life

I used to spend the term breaks with my mother, in mountainous places such as Wisla and Ustron, where there were spas and "miraculous" waters. While we were there, I would sit and watch the mud baths, my mother submerged up to her neck.

This went on until, one day, Mother decided to accept an invitation from a first cousin, for us to spend our vacation at his farm. Like my uncle, his name was Filip.

Vacations on the farm.
Part of the forty-strong family succumbed during the Holocaust. All died, with the exception of Mother, her brother, my stepfather, my half sister Kora, and me.

Mother told me that, since she was a teenager, this first cousin of hers had taken a special interest in her, but that the age difference between them (twelve years) together with the opposition of her family, who disapproved of relations between family members, had stifled the romance.

After this, Mother had married my father, and the cousin, Filip, fulfilled a promise he had made to a young girl he had met in Romania when he served there during the First World War, and he had married her. Her name was Lenutza Petresko.

She converted to Judaism before the wedding and went to live on Filip's enormous farm, Brzuska. Unfortunately, Lenutza contracted tuberculosis and died young, when her only child, Kora, was just thirteen years old.

One year after Lenutza's death, Filip and Mother married. And that was how I gained a stepfather and a sister.

Mother's Second Wedding

The wedding between my mother and Filip created a lot of discontent in me and Kora. For me, this discontent subsided only when I told myself that I now had a sister, whom I came to love unconditionally.

Delighted with the presents I had received from my future stepfather—such as a platinum ring with a small gem in the middle, and a pony, as well as skis, skates, and a sled—and excited by the enchanting and mysterious world of the farm, I gave my "permission" to my mother to marry.

I discovered that if my "uncle" (as I called him) had been good to us before the wedding, without doubt, he was even kinder after the wedding. But I never imagined that Mother would take my permission so seriously, to the point that she made up her mind very quickly.

At Mother's civil wedding. From right to left: Grandma, my stepfather, Mother, Edward, Ala, and Ala's intended.

Before the wedding, they went to consult a wise rabbi in the city of Dynów, since Mother had doubts about taking this step. The rabbi reassured her as to her fiancé's character and blessed them, but he required that they make a will, as each had a daughter, which was done.

On a morning like any other when I arrived home from school, I was quickly taken to one side by the housekeeper and dressed in a beautiful dress with an enormous ribbon shaped like a butterfly in my hair.

And that was how I discovered, without any prior warning, that there would be a party to celebrate my mother's wedding and that I should greet the newlyweds.

They had taken no heed of the threats that Kora and I had made that we would kill ourselves. Despite our "blackmail," they had married!

That was too much! On entering the room I ignored everyone, and instead of taking my place at the table, I simply took an armchair and pretended to read, by way of protest.

Nobody noticed me, except my uncle Filip, Mother's brother, who threw tinned mushrooms at the book in an attempt to play with me and improve my mood.

But nothing made any difference. At that moment, I was thinking about my father, alone somewhere, being replaced by another man who would never be my father, and whom I would never love like him.

In the afternoon when everyone was dancing in the living room of the apartment, I couldn't resist calling my friend Lídia to invite her to come and dance with me because I didn't have a partner. What a remedy!

For some time, I considered the "uncle" a usurper, despite his having been a loving stepfather, a true father. I accepted him more dearly only after my father died.

During the honeymoon in Brzuska. From left to right:
Mother, my stepfather, and my cousin Rusia.

While my father was alive, I never gave up the naïve hope that he and my mother would reconcile. In my mind, the man who had taken his place by her side had gone away, leaving Kora with me.

I Gained a Sister

The only thing that softened the blow of my mother's getting married was Kora, my stepfather's daughter. I was fascinated by her from the first moment I saw her.

She was and did everything that I wanted to be and do. She had beautiful long blonde braids, and she skated, skied, and climbed trees looking for nuts. She wore threadbare sneakers, her chest was covered by just a scarf secured at the back, and she wore faded shorts with a pocketknife in her belt. She used it to cut open frogs so that she could look inside, since she wanted to study medicine.

Kora at the end of the war.

Kora had a very strict upbringing. At mealtimes she was not permitted to participate in her parents' conversation or even to ask the maid for a glass of water, but instead she was required to serve herself. I think this was why she became such an introverted person who suffered in silence even when she was hurt.

Her mother's sickness merely reinforced this trait. For fear of Kora contracting tuberculosis, which was practically incurable at that time, she was prohibited from approaching the room where her mother lay.

As Kora was seven years older than me, we didn't have a lot of common interests back then, but with the passing of time this age difference no longer mattered, and we became very good friends and companions.

We also had different personalities, but this didn't affect our relationship or the tenderness that we felt for each other in any way. After our parents married, we considered ourselves blood sisters, even though we were only second cousins.

And talking of kinship, Kora had lighthearted flings with Edmund, Filip, and Edward,—Mother's three brothers— one after another.

When her daughter was born many years later, she gave her the names of the two grandmothers: Clara Elena, but the nickname Rita, since both Kora and my dear brother-in-law, Olek, thought that when Rita was small and just a teen, she was more like me in her behavior than like her mother. But this similarity disappeared over time.

A Fantastic World

At the farm, everything was magical and totally new to a young girl raised in the city ... who still believed in the stork and thus left sugar on her windowsill in the hope that it would bring her a little brother.

The day began with all of the children in the family taking soaps and towels and running to the creek to take a bath, which, for me, was something deliciously new.

We had many ways to amuse ourselves: we rehearsed plays such as *Hänsel and Gretel*, *Cinderella*, or *Little Red Riding Hood*. Later, we invited the adults to watch the spectacle, and they paid a token entrance fee: ten cents and a pear. The "audience" were always very generous with their applause.

One time, we held a country parade, which was common at the farm, with a bride and groom, groomsmen who played beautiful music, and the guests as extras. As the family was very large, we meandered, house by house, through the farm seeking gifts. Today's *festas juninas* (June festivals in Brazil) remind me a lot of these parades.

On rainy days, we played every type of game, such as patience, rummy, dominoes, checkers, hopscotch, and the wonderful *skakanka* (or *pulanka*, which I later adapted to teach my children and grandchildren). It's a version of the game of checkers in which the objective is to capture your opponent's territory by jumping his pieces, but without removing them as in checkers.

The hives full of honey, produced by hundreds of bees bent on stinging anyone who approached them, were another sideshow, albeit observed from a safe distance. Once, while attempting to lift out a honeycomb, my stepfather was stung on the upper lip, despite his protective headwear, and the lip swelled so much that it covered his nostrils for several days.

Another spectacle for me was the cows being milked by the farmworkers, with the milk swirling around in the buckets. On average, each cow produced between forty-two and fifty pints of milk per day. Watching the farmhands work made me want to have a go at milking, since it seemed easy, but it was a disaster: I took a "slap" from the cow's foul-smelling tail that almost knocked me off the stool. I was glad that the tail was dry, at least. It was my first and only experience of milking …

One day I had a fright. I was playing in the field with two cousins, Cyla and Ninia, when suddenly there appeared dozens of cows and steers heading back to the stable. The cousins, who were used to this, disappeared quickly and easily up a tree, while I stood petrified with nowhere to run.

I saw a little bridge made of two narrow wooden boards, about ten feet above the creek. I figured that there I would be safe, as a four-legged animal like a steer or a cow wouldn't be able to cross two such narrow planks.

I ran to the middle of this "fool's sanctuary" of a bridge and waited for the herd to pass. But I was outsmarted. I didn't even realize that I was wearing a red polka-dot dress. Suddenly, one of the steers broke off from the herd and calmly started to walk in my direction onto the bridge, probably attracted by the color of my dress.

It stepped onto the boards carefully, placing one foot behind the other, so as not to fall. The weight and movement of the animal caused the bridge to sway and me to lose my balance. I fell into the creek. Soaking wet, I looked up anxiously, but luckily the steer didn't jump. It just looked at me as if it was surprised to see me fall.

Back home, shaken and wet, I was still scolded by Mother for getting the dress dirty and not taking care of myself. That's how it went. Mother was very severe and, in my opinion, unfair at times. Whenever I fell or scraped my knee, she would first disinfect the wound and apply a dressing. After that, she would spank me so that I would learn to walk more carefully and not fall over anymore.

Childhood Innocence

Living on the farm, I was continually surprised by things that would be quite mundane to anyone who had grown up there. Everything was a novelty, like the day when I was walking near the stables and saw a newborn calf struggling to stay on its feet next to its mother, with the placenta still hanging from the cow's body.

Imagine what passed through my mind. I asked myself a thousand questions without coming up with an answer, unless it was that the cow was sick and the little calf, her son, had come to visit her.

When I saw the bulls mounting the cows, Mother, seeing my confusion, explained to me that this was how married animals kissed …

Exuberant Nature

Sometimes my stepfather took me on the back of the horse to inspect the harvest in the fields. The farmhands stopped and greeted him with their hats in their hands.

The enormity of the expanse of fields and forests that unraveled before my eyes made me feel free.

Another experience that delighted me was going into the orchard, which was full of the aroma of succulent fruit. I remember the strawberries in particular, pale in the morning but already ripe and red by the end of the afternoon, ready for me to savor. I was in heaven with that wonderful array of fresh fruit to be gathered in the orchard, which in the city didn't exist.

The branches of the trees strained under the weight of the apples, pears, and plums, and along the whole of the fence there were bushes full of *agrest* (gooseberries) and *pozeczki* (red currants)—succulent fruit that don't exist in Brazil—not to mention the sunflowers lined up like soldiers, which seemed to invite children to savor their seeds.

During the night, with the arrival of winter, the trunks of the trees in the orchard were tied down and protected from the cold, snow, and wind with straw. As the winters in Poland were very severe, reaching minus twenty degrees Celsius, the workers kept bonfires going every thirty feet between the trees to heat the air.

The farm was modern. There was mains electricity, hydraulic plumbing, a tennis and volleyball court, and a table-tennis table. On the lake, we sailed in a wooden boat that my stepfather had ordered built, which was named Nusia after the sweet nickname given to my mother.

Once a week, a band of musicians from the city of Bircza

was hired, and we would dance. For me, this was divine, since dancing had always been part of my life, and music my constant companion even today. It would make me emotional, sometimes to the point of tears.

Although there were various *fíakers* (carriages) on the farm, a new coach was built to my mother's specifications. That is, the distance between the first and second steps was designed so that Mother could climb up without difficulty.

I've no need to add that my stepfather simply worshipped my Mother. Moreover, Kora noticed that her father had never spoiled her mother the way that he spoiled mine, which was probably true.

The winter changed the aspect of the farm, and we skated on the frozen lake. The adults played ice hockey, respecting the rules of the game. Only Uncle Filip played without skates, running after the puck in felt boots. It was so comical that even he laughed. In the mountains, the guests skied, led by Kora. She skied wearing only long pants and a checked flannel shirt with the sleeves rolled up.

Uncle Filip playing hockey.

In the forests, hunts were organized. I remember the forest rangers with their dogs, blowing trumpets to drive the prey into the range of the hunters, who were invited from neighboring farms.

The path to the forest was a sleigh trail lined with bearskins (the products of previous hunts). Mother and I traveled in comfort, and Kora and the cousins followed behind on skis, holding on to leather ropes tied to the sleigh. While we waited to see the results of the hunt, a group of farmhands lit a bonfire to roast meat, potatoes, nuts, and other delicacies that we ate after a hunt.

For us children, coming down the mountain on a sled was an adventure, especially when the sled tipped over and we fell into a snowbank. Delicious!

I smile to think of my mother's telling me that when she was a child, she and a friend came down a steep, craggy mountain on a sled at high speed. They were unable to avoid a small cabin at the foot of the hill, with snow up to its windows, and they went through an open window and landed on a bed, startling the terrified farmhands inside.

Request Denied

One day father came to visit me at the farm and made a request of my mother. He wanted me to live with him, as he felt very lonely and missed me. He also mentioned that there was someone new in his life whom he wanted to marry, but he made it clear that he would forego the marriage in order to dedicate himself to me, if Mother agreed to let me live with him.

After listening to him patiently, Mother advised him to marry again and rebuild his life, since she was never going to place me in his care. But she reassured him that, whenever he wanted, he could visit me unannounced and take me for a walk, as he did on alternate vacations.

Before he said good-bye, Father—despite his distress at being denied—remembered to remind me not to get too close to people who had had contact with Kora's mother, as I might catch something.

To this day, I remember the look of sadness he wore that day.

Vacations with Father, Before the War

The last winter vacations that I spent with Father before the war were wonderful. We were in Wisla. He gave me his complete attention, calling me "my little girlfriend."

We came down the mountains on a sled at night at amazing speeds. After dinner, Father entertained the hotel guests with his marvelous, and renowned, sense of humor, telling jokes, and doing impressions and magic tricks. I felt very proud seeing how much people enjoyed the fun, clapping and asking for encores.

He was an expert dancer, almost as good as a professional. He was my teacher and my "accomplice," since I told him everything that passed between my mother and her husband, mercilessly.

I described the jewelry that Mother received from her husband, and repeated the declarations of love that he made and the pet names that they called each other. I acted this way to make my father jealous, so that he would feel the need to fight for Mother and bring her back to him. The imagination and desires of children know no bounds when it comes to getting what they want.

When Father came to visit my grandparents' house, he wasted no time in putting a disc on the gramophone, and we would dance every type of dance: minuet, rumba, Viennese waltz, English waltz, tango, foxtrot, slow fox, and, naturally, the polka.

As Father lived in Warsaw, we spent little time together, but they were always marvelous and unforgettable occasions, because it was just the two of us. He usually took me to the candy store, and while I tried the delicious treats, we chatted and made plans for our vacations.

Before I could read and write, the letters that I received from him were drawn in pictures so I could understand what we were going to do for the next vacation from the illustrations.

When the Sky
Began to Fall In

The anti-Semitic protests in the city of Katowice began in 1939.

In front of my grandfather's chain of stores, pejorative pamphlets were distributed inciting the population not to buy from Jewish establishments, with rhyming slogans such as "*Nie kupuj u zyda to najlepsza rada, kto kupuje u zyda ten sam siebie okrada*" (Follow this advice—don't buy from a Jew's store; buying from a Jew just makes you poor) or "*Precz z zydami, zydowki z nami!*" (Jews go away, but your women can stay!).

At school, a colleague called Misio Landau and I were the only Jews from Szkolna Road. He was the scapegoat for everything bad that happened in the class, and the other children pointed to him as being responsible for any misbehavior. But he was never the guilty one, being quiet and shy, sitting at the back of the class by the wall.

The teacher, Jan Obraczka, laid him facedown on the front desk and beat him with a ruler. I asked myself why he never complained to his parents, and why they never placed him in a Jewish school.

The Jewish families had a certain pride in sending their children and grandchildren to public schools, where only the Jews from important families were admitted.

I was the teacher's "pet" because I was at the top of the class and spoke Polish with good diction. Thus I was often asked, on behalf of the school, to recite the many tributes made to the director.

At school in 1938–39.
In the background, Misio Landau, who was the class scapegoat.

There was one occasion, on the birthday of Ignacy Moscicki, the Polish president at that time, that I recited a poem on the radio, on the famous children's program *Aunt Fela*. I went, but the teacher, Jan, warned me ahead of time that because I didn't have a typical Polish surname, I would be announced just as Rita. The tenor of the poem was as follows:

*Panie Prezydencie w dniu Twojego swieta
stoi tu gromadka dzieci usmiechnieta,
i z tych wszystkich dzieci kazde jedno powie
Niech Ci Bog da szczescie; niech Ci Bog da zdrowie.
Niech nad calym krajem slonko jasno swieci,
Niech u dobrych ludzi, rosna zdrowe dzieci.*

Mr. President, the children party this day,
And with their smiles they say,
May God give him health; may God give him happiness.
May the sun smile on our homeland, in all its greatness.
And in every home,
May healthy children roam.

All the members of the family stood around the radio, thrilled to listen to my recital, and when I got home, I received some golden coins, both as a reward and for luck.

For the Jewish High Holidays, such as Rosh Hashanah[2] and Yom Kippur[3], the teacher, Jan Obraczka, visited our house to find out why I was absent from school. I was quickly put to bed with some swaddling cloth around my neck to prove that I had the flu, as we had been prohibited from being absent on these dates.

Despite this, my fondness for Jan Obraczka was undiminished, as he justified himself by saying that he was only following the orders of the director of the school.

When the class went to the circus, he always put me in a box seat next to himself and his girlfriend, while the other pupils sat in the crowd.

My fondness for this teacher ended the day that he punished me unfairly. At that time, we had to keep our hands behind our backs whenever we weren't reading or writing. But one time, simply because I was distracted, I put my hands on my desk, and so it happened: the teacher called me to his desk and punished me by caning my palms twice with a ruler in front of the whole class. Not content with this, he made me face the blackboard for the rest of the class. The shame that I felt killed all the admiration that I had for him.

---

2   Rosh Hashanah: Jewish New Year.
3   Yom Kippur: Day of Forgiveness (or Day of Atonement). One of Judaism's most important celebrations. A period given over to deep reflection and regret, and to each individual's commitment to become a better human being.

Forced Break

When the priest entered the class to give catechism, Misio Landau and I were obliged to leave, because we were not allowed to attend religious classes.

We spent an hour aimlessly walking or running along the corridors of the school. When we returned to the classroom, our classmates looked at us with irony and suspicion, and I felt uncomfortable but tried to hide it.

Before classes began, the pupils made a sign of the cross and prayed the Our Father, standing next to their desks. As a sign of respect, the two of us kept quiet, also standing. It didn't bother me that we behaved differently from the Christian pupils, but having to leave the classroom because we were Jews was hard to take.

We were curious to hear the catechism simply because it was forbidden. This, among other things, was one of the manifestations of anti-Semitism that we faced. Only later did we learn that the priest was inciting the children to hate the Jews, because we were considered deicides, responsible for the death of Jesus.

At that time, what the cleric omitted was that Jesus was born, lived, and was buried within the Jewish religion, also having been circumcised seven days after he was born, according to Jewish custom. To sow the seeds of hate between the religions, the priests didn't teach that the crucifixion took place at the order of the Romans, as history tells it, but attributed the blame to the Jews.

When a Polish child was asked why she didn't like the Jews, she invariably replied, "I don't know!", something that has continued up to the present day, with numerous cases of unfounded prejudice.

Jewish Life before the War

In general, anti-Semitism could be felt in the air, but it wasn't always obvious. But, as I said before, none of this prevented me from being happy—very happy.

At this time, some Semite families hired a Polish Jewish teacher to give us private classes about the Jewish religion and the history of our ancestry, in a classroom donated by another college.

Despite the indications of hostility against the Jews, we could never have imagined that, in the near future, there would be the tragedy of the Holocaust. Poland was our homeland, and we were patriots, even though we were treated as undesirable tenants by most people.

Even with the anti-Semitic demonstrations, the Jewish community of Katowice was perfectly integrated into society as a whole, going to concerts, theaters, cinemas, candy stores, and night clubs, actively supporting charity events.

We received many newspapers at home, always in the Polish language.

When there were major festivals, the temple was filled with elegantly dressed ladies in hats, jewelry, and other adornments, such as a flower pinned to the dress, following the fashion of the day. The men wore dark suits and ties, leading their sons and grandsons solemnly by the hand. On the day of fasting, I presented my grandmother with a bouquet of flowers.

The Celebrations at Home

The nights of *Pesach*[4] were nights of unbridled joy. My three uncles, all of them single, led the festivities, breaking hard-boiled eggs on each other's heads, to the total disgust of my grandfather, who prayed and pretended to see nothing.

At the suggestion of my grandfather Salo, who made a point of always keeping the doors of our house open to show that nothing untoward was going on inside, we frequently invited Christian students and colleagues of my uncles.

The last Passover celebration before the war, in 1939.
From the left: Kora, Uncle Filip, Mother, my stepfather,
Aunt Ala, Grandpa, me, and Grandma.

---

4   Passover: Jewish Easter. Celebrates and remembers the liberation of the people of Israel from Egypt.

With this initiative, my grandfather also wanted to show that the *matzá* (unleavened bread) was not made from the blood of Christian children, as some fathers told their children, and as cruel anti-Semitic fancy would have it.

This, and other attitudes of my grandfather, clearly demonstrated how he was a liberal and intelligent Jew, a Polish citizen who kept the rituals of his religion as well as an open mind, at a time when many Jewish families behaved in a more traditional and closed manner, especially in the small cities.

For me, the part I most looked forward to was the search for the *aficoman*, a piece of *matzá* hidden by an adult to encourage the children to wait for the end of *Seder*[5] (Passover Seder). Whoever found it could choose a present. As I was the only child in the family, I didn't need to share the present with anyone. Grandma Berta was my accomplice, as she'd point to where Grandpa had hidden the *matzá*.

When it came to choosing the present, I'd ask for shoes, as Grandpa was the owner of a chain of shoe stores. It wasn't exactly what I most wanted, but as they didn't give me any option, I played along.

For *Shabbat*[6], when Grandma Berta lit the candles, I was always by her side. I don't know why, but I had the impression that when she lit them, Grandma's face took on a look of sadness, while she whispered a prayer.

---

5   Seder: Passover dinner.
6   Shabbat or Sabbath: weekly day of rest observed from sunset on Friday until sunset on Saturday. According to Jewish tradition, it is inspired by the divine rest on the seventh day of Creation.

At the *Hanukkah*[7] festival, which lasted eight days, a candelabra with eight candles was lit.

For Christmas, Grandfather permitted a tree to be set up with colored balls, so that the employees in the house might celebrate the date in the Christian tradition. In addition, one of the employees dressed up as Santa Claus and carried an enormous sack full of presents, which they shared with me.

Grandfather explained that the origin of Santa Claus was an old man called Nicholas who lived in a small town in Finland, and who was so kind that in December he gave out presents to the children in the village.

The visit of Santa Claus, by design, always took place during dinner. My plate would be full, with the menu invariably being creamed spinach with two fried eggs on top and mashed potatoes.

Normally, I hated spinach and refused to eat it, but faced with Santa Claus I forgot everything and simply devoured the lot, the nanny struggling to fill the spoon quickly enough to keep up.

By way of thanks for all of the presents I received, I recited a poem in German, which was the mother tongue of the old man and which I knew because we had lived in Upper Silesia.

Ich bin klein main,
Hertz ist rein,
zoll niemand drin;
vohnen als Herr Got alain.

---

7   Hanukkah (dedication) Jewish celebration also known as the Festival of Lights. It begins at sunset on the 24th day of the Jewish month *Kislev* and is celebrated for eight days.

I am a seed,
A heart yet to bleed,
Which only God can fill;
I know no other will.

Grandfather Salo also didn't object to the nanny's taking me to church once in a while on Sundays. He explained that there was no harm in this, and he also didn't criticize the entrance of non-Jews into the synagogues.

His only advice was for me not to kneel in front of any image—given that we believed in the one God—and that I should stand back when the faithful were kneeling, as a mark of respect.

Thus, all of the taboos were always dealt with wisely. Tolerance and harmony were ever present in our house.

A Sharp Sense of Humor

After the divorce my father, when he came, continued to stay at the house of my maternal grandparents. The relationship between him and my uncles also remained very friendly, strengthened by the sense of humor that they shared.

When Father came from Warsaw to seek me out for our vacations, he stayed in the guest room right up to the day we set off, even after my mother married again.

They were always moments of great happiness, pleasure, and tenderness. He would take me for walks and to eat ice-cream and was very affectionate, kissing me on the cheeks and asking, "Ritusia kochusia tatusia?" (My little Rita loves her Daddy?). To which I replied, "Tak, Ritusia kochusia *bardzo* tatusia." (Yes, little Rita loves Daddy *very much*.)

I remember one night when I was lying down with my grandmother. She used to read me stories from comic books. Suddenly, the door opened to reveal three Bedouins with bath towels tied around their waists and turbans on their heads. It was my uncles, of course!

With their faces painted with charcoal, and false beards and mustaches, they writhed and twisted in an attempt to perform a belly dance. To complete the spectacle, they began to play music with the help of some instruments that they had brought along: Uncle Edmund played a comb with crepe paper as a type of kazoo, Uncle Filip provided percussion on a drum, and Uncle Edward clashed two saucepan lids and sang. They all beat in time, and in harmony with the masterfully executed melody of Uncle Edmund.

Needless to say, my grandparents and I enjoyed the scene enormously, roaring with laughter.

Other Hilarious Stories

At that time, it was customary for the *chatchn*[8] to arrange marriages for the single girls or divorced ladies of important families.

The matchmakers wore a black suit and cloak, which were sometimes threadbare, a hat, and the inseparable umbrella, which was also part of the wardrobe of the female matchmakers.

Once the marriage that they arranged was over, they received—usually from the family of the bride—a preestablished sum of money, which was why they always made an extra effort.

And it was this that led to another hilarious episode. When Mother and Aunt Ala were both divorced, a *chatchn* showed up at the house, much to the disgust of my grandparents, since the daughters of Salo and Berta Blum would never deign to meet the supposed marital prospects suggested by a *chatchn*.

When the poor man showed up, we couldn't help but notice that the zipper of his pants was half-open, and there appeared to be something resembling a salami or a sausage poking out. My indignant grandmother almost fainted at the matchmaker's affront, and she wasted no time in covering my eyes and ordering me from the room.

I don't know what they talked about, but after a few minutes I heard everybody roaring with laughter, and I ran back in to find out what was happening. And imagine

---

8   *Chatchn*: matchmakers.

what I saw: the man was in fact my father, dressed up to perfection, so that even my grandparents didn't recognize him. Finally, he cut the string of sausages and tore off the beard and mustache, and everybody laughed long and hard.

That was my father—outgoing and charming, with a special sense of humor. While not handsome, he captivated everyone with his ability to impersonate, and he built such a rapport that even after the divorce, his former in-laws continued to like him, much to my pleasure.

Part Two: The War

The Invasion of the Soviet Troops

It was September 1939 when our vacation at the Brzuska farm (our last there, although we didn't know it at the time) was interrupted by the war. Everything happened so unexpectedly that it seemed like the world had fallen in on my family and me.

One sunny afternoon in October, I was lying with my cousins on the lawn that circled the farmhouse. We were playing a game in which we would stare at the clouds and win points for finding the most objects or animals in the shapes that the clouds formed.

Suddenly, we heard the roar of an engine in the sky and soon after saw a plane flying low over the farm, giving us the impression that it was reconnoitering the area. It flew so low that we were able to see the head of the pilot through the window of the plane, which soon disappeared into the distance.

We were surprised because we had never seen a plane in the skies above Brzuska, but we didn't attach any great significance to it. Later we heard the adults discussing the event.

A few days later, a messenger arrived at the neighboring farms in a hurry, warning us that the Russian troops had invaded, having crossed the frontier of Poland, and that they were deporting the *burjui* (landowners, in Russian) to Siberia. After plundering everything, the soldiers distributed the land and whatever was left to the peasants.

Wasting no time, the farmworkers, guided by my stepfather, prepared seven large carts, each pulled by two horses, loaded up with enough nonperishable provisions for at least ten days of travel.

There were tins of butter, cheese, honey, and jam; sacks of flour, sugar, rye bread, white bread, and cookies; preserved meats; roasted poultry; cooked eggs; and all types of fruit.

In the middle of the carts, clothes and blankets were gathered and covered with a waterproof canvas. Each cart was driven by a pair of adults, who took turns driving.

In our cart, a small space was created for me in the middle of the hay, right behind my mother and stepfather, covered by a blanket for sleeping, as we were leaving at night and the temperatures in October got very cold, especially at night.

Before we left, Pedro, a trusted family employee, helped us to bury all of our crystal, gold, and silverware, and animal skins such as foxes and others were preserved in zinc caskets.

The Persian rugs were rolled up and placed in aluminum tubes and wooden boxes, which were wrapped in linoleum and finally buried in deep trenches.

Pedro suggested that Mother stay behind to look after everything, promising to offer every protection until we returned. Needless to say, no one thought much of this idea.

The time arrived for us to depart.

My stepfather's cart led the caravan, with him driving and my mother at his side, and me lying down under a sky full of stars, which seemed to come along with us.

Next came the cart carrying Kora and a cousin, and so on. The seven carts left the farm under the dark of night to escape the bombers.

Looking back now on these events, I'm surprised that

I wasn't frightened by the situation. On the contrary, I felt like I was part of a curious adventure.

From time to time, Mother checked with her hand to see if I had slid out from the hay. One night, my stepfather fell asleep while steering the horses, and our cart left the road, almost plunging into a ditch. From then on, Mother shared the driving with him.

We thought that the Russians would soon retreat, and everything would return to normal, and we would go back to the farm. We could never have imagined that we would never return.

We learned later that soon afterward, the Russians invaded our farm, and Pedro was the first to show them where our families' valuables were buried. And all this was accompanied by shouts and cries of, "Welcome! Finally you've arrived!"

The Flight

We wandered for eight days and eight nights. During the day we hid the carts in the woods so that they wouldn't be spotted by aircraft, which bombed anything that moved. The horses were left to roam the fields. When there were no creeks nearby, my family searched out houses to ask for water for ourselves and our horses.

I remember that Aunt Ala and Kora "attacked" the sunflowers, removing their seeds and storing them in silk stockings. Sometimes we managed to help ourselves to fruit in the orchards of abandoned farms.

I recall that one day, in some square or other, we were sunbathing along with some cousins, when some planes appeared with soldiers who started shooting at the people.

Everyone scrambled desperately for somewhere to hide. I found myself alone in the middle of the square and ran to hide under a bench, which, to my dismay, was not big enough to cover me completely. I thus had to choose between hiding my head or my legs. I chose my head.

These were terrifying moments. After the planes disappeared, we gathered to see if anyone was hurt. Luckily, one of my uncles was saved by the wind: a bullet passed through his billowing shirt, without hitting him.

Our aim was to reach the city of Stanislavov, where a cousin of my stepfather, Uncle Munio Seibald, was the owner of a mill, and someone very important and respected in the city, by the Christians as well as the Jews. We planned to stay there until the Russians withdrew.

Along the way, we crossed a street with wounded Polish soldiers being supported by their comrades. They were beating a retreat, going in the opposite direction to ours to escape the front line.

It was then that there was an incident that I never forgot. A soldier approached us with his wife, and a child on her lap, and asked for a ride. Naturally we couldn't refuse.

Soon after, the bombing commenced. Everyone abandoned the carts on the street and hid themselves in the middle of a wheat field. The soldier gave the baby to my stepfather and went into hiding with his wife.

Suddenly, we saw my stepfather in the middle of the street, impotent, paralyzed with fear, with no idea what to do. Thankfully, he didn't move and wasn't hit. After the bombing, we all returned to the carts, and the couple collected their child and disappeared. Someone said later that they could have been spies to the Russian Government.

New Confiscations

When we arrived in a little village called Olesiov, close to Stanislavov, we stopped for a few days to rest. The place seemed like an oasis in the desert. Each family rented a room from the residents while we waited for news from Uncle Munio, whom we had sent a message that we were in the vicinity of the city of Stanislavov.

Soon after, a buggy arrived, sent by my uncle Munio with four armed Jewish civilians aboard, who would escort us to Stanislavov, as it was very dangerous to travel there without protection. Attacks had become frequent in what was now a "no man's land."

Reaching the city, we parked up on the enormous courtyard of Uncle Munio's mill. A few hours later, some Russian officials arrived and promptly confiscated all of the horses, leaving us with just the carts.

Some days later, my stepfather broke down in tears when he saw a contingent of soldiers heading for the front and recognized his horse, *Siwka* (Gray), among those pulling the gun batteries.

After a little while, I got to know two sisters, Rozia and Fredzia Eisner, who lived with their father and stepmother in front of the mill. I became good friends with them, especially Fredzia, who, miraculously, was the only one saved out of her entire family. When the parents and sister were later deported with the other Jews, she was spending some time with an aunt in a village somewhere.

Nowadays, Fredzia lives in Haifa, Israel, and is married to Moshe Katz, a lawyer. Some thirty years later, we met again when I visited Israel with my husband, Mauricio, and it was a very emotional occasion, as neither of us knew that the other had survived.

Setting Up Home in Stanislavov

Our family decided to stay in Stanislavov while we waited for the Soviet forces to withdraw and allow us to go home. How deluded we were!

But life didn't seem so bad, at least not to my eyes.

With no freedom of expression, we had to agree with everything and wildly applaud what was said at the so-called *mitings*, weekly meetings that took place in the social rooms of the buildings, where the invaders indoctrinated the people.

As being a landowner (*burjui*) was considered a crime, punishable with deportation to Siberia, my stepfather altered his documents to replace the word "landowner" with "worker."

Many times during the night, Russian authorities appeared, checking the documents and looking for the "alias" Filip Ringel.

Surprising Habits

Living with the Russian troops wasn't easy. The soldiers were primitive and assaulted people on the street with the sole objective of stealing their wristwatch to wear it later with the sleeves rolled up, as a status symbol.

To obtain some rubles (Russian currency), Mother started selling some personal items to the wives of officials, such as long satin negligees and silk stockings.

Imagine our amazement at seeing these ladies going to the theater wearing Mother's negligees as prom dresses, with leather jackets over them. They were accompanied by their ostentatiously dressed husbands, sporting uniforms with countless medals on their chests and carrying children in their arms.

We also witnessed a scene in a bathroom where a soldier flushed the toilet and washed his face in the gushing water.

This is not to mention how, in the absence of vodka, they contented themselves with drinking the eau de cologne they had confiscated from us.

Countless other examples such as these highlighted the lack of culture and knowledge of the youngsters whom I came across, who had been prematurely sent to war by the Russian army.

For example, on seeing mothers pushing their babies along in baby carriages, the Russians marveled at the number of "paraplegic" Polish children. They also wondered at the luxury of each bathroom having a little bathtub for washing the babies. They were referring to the bidets, of course.

Once, two soldiers entered a store selling Persian rugs which belonged to one of our friends. They liked one rug in particular but realized that it was too big for the space they had in mind. The solution that they came up with was to ask the storekeeper to cut the rug in half. Thus they left satisfied, each with half of the rug rolled up under one arm.

Valuing Talent

On the other hand, the Russian authorities encouraged and invested in children with artistic abilities, offering scholarships for courses in dance, singing, recital, and musical instruments.

The director of our school received the order to nominate three girls or boys who were talented in such arts to attend classes at the "Palace of Culture," free of charge.

As luck would have it, he nominated three Jewish girls: Lunia Gotlib for the recital classes, Ninia Rosenblat for the singing classes, and me for the ballet classes. In the end, he also nominated a fourth child, a boy whose name I don't recall, for the violin classes.

I remember these classes vividly for the teacher, who had an extraordinary Russian talent for the ballet and popular dance, and especially for the quality of the teaching. The dance compositions that he taught us to perform were fantastically choreographed, creative, and varied, including both group and solo dances.

In one of these performances, we danced with our backs to the audience, wearing masks with the faces of old ladies, scarves draped around our heads from which gray hair tumbled down, with long aprons and our arms crossed behind our backs, imitating *babuskas* (grandmothers, in Russian). Our deliberately uncoordinated movements produced a comic effect. The twist was saved for the end, when we turned around and gracefully pulled aside the aprons to reveal our shorter skirts, and appeared with our young faces.

Me, dressed as a gentleman in a dinner jacket waiting for a girlfriend, in a choreography created by the Russian dance teacher.

We performed two other compositions in pairs, in which I also took part, as well as a solo for the Viennese waltz "Blue Danube," by Johann Strauss.

The most exciting part of these classes was that, after many rehearsals, we took part in a competition against other schools. The winner received a prize. As it happened, Lunia Gotlib won the prize in the recital category, Ninia Rosenblat won the singing, and I won the ballet.

I remember Lunia's poem and Ninia's singing even today. Sadly, these two talented girls didn't survive the Holocaust, swelling the list of many other talented individuals murdered by the Nazis. After the Russians retreated, we never saw each other again, but their memory lives on forever.

Under Russian Rule

In the schools, we were subjected to true brainwashing. All of the crucifixes were taken down from the walls of the classrooms (Poland is a predominantly Catholic country), and they were replaced with portraits of Marshall Josef Stalin.

They also advised the students to pray silently, according to each religion, to ask God for candy. Crazy for anything sweet, I prayed fervently, but in vain, as nothing happened.

Next, they instructed us to pray aloud in unison to *Batko* (father, in Russian) Stalin and—lo and behold!—the doors opened and two workers entered carrying an enormous basket full of cookies, chocolates, lollipops, and sugar candy, promptly shared among the classmates.

I remember the taste of some gingerbread covered in chocolate. It was simply heavenly. After the candies were handed out, came the question: "Tell me: Does God exist?"

And we replied aloud, "God doesn't exist."

"So who, then, is our God?"

"Batko Stalin is our god."

To avoid possible deportation, a fate that was common, and to demonstrate my adherence to communism, I joined the youth movement *Pioner*. I wore a red scarf around my neck, learned the raised fist salute, and sang patriotic songs, whose melodies happened to be very beautiful. Even so, my singing distressed my stepfather enormously.

Kora, for her part, joined *Kosmol*, a movement for young people over fifteen years old.

At the meetings, which were obligatory, we applauded

each speaker and agreed with everything that he or she preached. If someone didn't applaud enthusiastically, he or she was singled out and later taken for interrogation at the NKWD headquarters, the Russian secret police, later called the KGB. Often, this interrogation was accompanied by mental torture.

Once, when Mother was selling a pair of socks at a street market, she was taken by two soldiers to the secret police. Despite the fact that the socks belonged to her, she was accused of trading, which was illegal under the communist regime.

After many exhausting hours of interrogation, Mother was released late at night. My stepfather and I waited desperately, worried to death, as we knew that often, once people were taken to the NKWD, they never returned, not even to say good-bye, being deported directly to Siberia.

Mother returned exhausted and covered in mud, as in the darkness she had fallen into a ditch. When she arrived, we were overjoyed to see her safe and sound.

At this time, in the beginning of 1941, Father came to seek me out so that we could go to the city of Lvov, where he lived with his wife and seven-month-old son, Oscar. He missed me and wanted to introduce me to his new family, and to have his two children together for a few days. Mother greeted him cordially as always, and we slept in my bedroom until it was time to leave.

Early in the morning, when I noticed that my mother was taking a bath, I called Father over to spy on her through the keyhole, in the hope that he would fall in love with her once again and we three could all return together. Obviously, he didn't accept my invitation and even told my mother of my scheme.

I still dreamed that Father, despite being married, would abandon his wife to come back and live with us, because one day I had seen a photograph of my mother fall from his pocket. He had quickly stepped on the photo, with his finger on his lips, urging me to keep quiet. I was enthralled by what I had seen and, of course, kept the secret.

On meeting my father's wife, Póla, I immediately disliked her, but I adored my little brother.

Some days after I arrived, Father took me to visit an aunt of his, a very old lady. Before we went in, he warned me that everyone who visited kissed her hand, but I didn't need to do so. When I asked why, he told me that the Hitners greeted one another with respect and kissed only on the cheek.

My parents had agreed that after two weeks I would return to my mother in Stanislavov.

Unfortunately, and quite unexpectedly, the Russians retreated from the city of Lvov, where we were, and then the German army conquered the city.

I was sick, fearing that I would never see my mother again. I had a high fever and stomach pains. Father forced me to calm down and gave me what medicine he had at home. But the days passed, and there was no sign that the Russian forces would return to the city.

The German Army's Presence in Lvov

Immediately, Jews began to be persecuted and deported. Father's three cousins, who lived with their families in our apartment, were taken by truck to perform "forced labor." Father escaped only because, at the last moment, thanks to his agility, he hid himself in the upper section of a closet, behind a pile of bedclothes.

At night, the cousins returned, tired, bloodied, and appalled, and told how they were obliged to dig graves to bury the bodies of the oldest men, who had been summarily shot.

The following day, one of them, cousin Izio, didn't return. The family was beginning the seven-day mourning period when he returned, covered in blood and lime, looking like a ghost. He described how he had been made to join a single file of five people and was ordered to lean toward the grave so that he would fall into it after he was shot.

This was a common procedure among the Germans. To save bullets, they would shoot the first in the line and hit all the rest.

Cousin Izio wasn't hurt, but he jumped into the ditch with the others. He stayed under the bodies until nightfall, and when the guards and their Ukrainian collaborators left for the night, having thrown some lime onto the bodies, with a great effort he managed to extract himself and climb out, using the bodies for support.

His speech was very disjointed as he told the story, and it became clear that he was disoriented. And he stayed this way for many days.

Father was invited to work in the courtyard of the Gestapo, shining the boots of the soldiers. Once I came across him by chance on the street close to where we lived, and I saw that he was delivering armfuls of helmets and boots that dangled from both arms. To my sadness, I noticed that he seemed very uncomfortable with the situation.

The Ghetto in Lvov

The day arrived when the truck pulled up in front of a neighboring building to take the Jews who lived there to a newly built ghetto, which was raised in record time, and which was surrounded by walls and electric fences.

To the shouts of the soldiers and the barking of their dogs, the residents of the building descended the steps, running in the direction of the street. Wasting no time, soldiers armed with rifles herded them into line with rifles, and the Jews entered the truck surrounded by Germans shouting, "Louse ferfluchte, Juden." (Quickly, stinking Jews.)

When the truck stopped in front of our building, the scene was repeated: the Germans shouted through loudspeakers, pressing us. The dogs barked fiercely, and we heard the cries of the victims, who, shoved violently by the rifles, stumbled and often fell.

It was our turn ...

The Jews were obliged to wear an armband with the Star of David. This is the armband I used in the ghetto.

A Choice That Broke
My Heart

We grabbed only what we could carry and stepped out into the street, two steps at a time. The line for the truck was long. We joined the end of the line and waited for our turn to board. I took a fearful glance at the fierce dogs baring their teeth, trained to rip pieces off their victims whenever the word *jude!* (Jew) was shouted out.

The first to enter the truck was Póla, who carried Oscar on her lap. Next up, Father put his bags onto the truck next to mine. When he bent down to pick me up and put me in the truck, we heard a shout, "Edmund Hitner!" I don't know who called out, if it was the Germans or a very well-dressed Christian gentleman, who introduced himself as Urban and offered Father a letter, which he read quickly.

In the letter, Mother explained that she had hired Mr. Urban so that he could take me to join her. Half of the amount agreed for the service had already been paid. The other half would be paid as soon as I arrived safely.

In the face of German protests about his approaching the Jews, Urban explained that I was his niece, a Christian, and that I was thus with the group of Jews by mistake.

Despite the drama around him, which could have ended in tragedy, Father crouched beside me to look in my eyes and said, "Darling, this letter is from Mommy. She has asked me to put you in the care of this gentleman, who has been paid to take you back to her. In Stanislavov, as far as we know, there is no ghetto yet. I don't know which of us will survive this war or if any of us will survive. This is why, my darling, it's up to you to decide if you wish to go with him or to go with us to the ghetto. I cannot and should not decide for you. It is your life and your choice too. Know that, whatever you decide, Daddy is not going to be hurt or sad."

After hearing these words, I had to decide my life in a matter of seconds. There was no time to think about it.

The Germans were already losing patience with us and threatening us with rifles. Póla was sitting in the truck with the baby in her arms, waiting for Father, who in turn was waiting for my decision.

With my father's words still ringing in my ears, that he wouldn't be sad, I replied, shyly, in barely a whisper, "So I'll go to meet Mommy."

At that moment, we couldn't even say good-bye. Mr. Urban removed me from the line and took me away from this terrible scene. Before we left, however, he gave Father the address of the inn where we were going to spend the night to wait for the train.

This scene remains clearly etched on my memory. When I think of it, I still feel an emotion so strong, that it is as if it had just happened.

Good-bye to My Father

I waited for Father at the window of the boardinghouse. When it got dark, I saw his slim figure hidden among the shade of the trees and the walls of the houses. He'd come to meet me. We hugged each other in silence for some minutes. Next, Father hung a small sack of coins around my neck and said, "If Mr. Urban denies you bread and water during the trip, buy what you can to feed yourself."

We kissed, promising that after the war we would meet again.

That was the last time that I saw him.

When Father walked away, I felt a shiver of fear at suddenly being alone in the world, depending on only a stranger who seemed very unfriendly, if not hostile.

The return trip to join up with my mother was tortuous. The bombers forced us to descend from the train many times to hide ourselves in the middle of the vegetation.

Whenever I asked Urban if I was close to being able to hug my mother, he answered by telling me not to get too excited, because we might be killed by a bomber.

When we finally arrived at the city, I was happy, as I felt safe. But Urban told me that I still shouldn't get too excited, because I still might stumble and crack my head open. That was how he was: a cruel man, who did what he did just for a lot of money, with no sentiment or compassion.

Finally I arrived home. Mother was at a neighbor's house, listening to an underground radio station to find out the situation with the bombing of the trains. My stepfather, after hugging and kissing me, built up to sharing the news of my arrival, to prevent Mother from being overcome by shock and emotion. And that's what he did.

On speaking to Mother, he said only that he had received the news that I had arrived at the station. Mother wanted to run straight to meet me, but she was convinced to wait for me at home.

I was listening to this conversation, hidden behind the closet, and couldn't wait any longer. I ran out of hiding and into her arms, laughing and crying with happiness all at once. Nothing else mattered: not the bombers, not fear, not the war. It was as if we had merged into one person. Time stopped ... Unfortunately, the memory of my father, whom I had abandoned to face an uncertain future, kept filling my mind.

Just an Illusion

Life in the city under the rule of the occupying Russian army was difficult. But although crudely educated, when they began to retreat in the face of Hitler's troops, they had the decency to suggest to the population of the city that they leave Stanislavov and flee the German occupation with them.

Our family held a meeting and decided unanimously that we would stay and wait for the "erudite and civilized" Germans. German punctuality and hygiene were well known, and their culture had already given the world figures such as Bach, Goethe, Mozart, and many others.

Therefore, we decided that living under their rule would be easier and much better than living under the command of the Russian troops. What a delusion!

If only we'd boarded the trains with the Russian army. Incidentally, Kora had fallen in love with a Jewish communist, Lomo Frisz, and wanted to go with him. But my stepfather ran all the way to the train station and pulled her from the carriage, bringing her back home.

Test of Faith

One day when the bombers began, we saw Christians clutching their rosary beads, running to take shelter inside the churches, and Jews in *talit* [9] or carrying prayer books, seeking shelter in the synagogues. But Mother, without thinking twice, grabbed my hand and ran in the direction of the bunker.

I remember asking her why we didn't join those who had faith, and thus deserved to be saved. Her reply was blunt: "My darling, if God exists, he is somewhere else or has forgotten us. But he gave us the means to protect ourselves. We should stay hidden belowground, because the domes of the synagogues and the towers of the churches are easily seen by our enemies."

The following morning when the bombers finally ceased and we were able to leave the bunker, we saw the faithful bloody and buried under the wreckage of the churches and synagogues. Faced with this terrible scene, my confusion was enormous. I thought that God had been unfair to exactly those people who were much more worthy of his mercy than us. At that moment, my faith took a body blow.

---

9   Talit: a shawl worn during Jewish prayers. Masculine religious accessory similar to a lightweight shawl.

A Strategic Choice

It was no accident that Hitler chose Poland to invade first, in beginning the atrocities of the Holocaust. As well as sharing a border with Germany, the country was home to the largest number of Jews in Europe.

The dictator was also well aware that the anti-Semitism that reigned over the country would prove fertile ground for accomplishing what he intended to do, providing endless collaborators. And that is what happened, to the extent that some of the survivors today consider Poland as "the cemetery for the final remains of the Jews."

Many Poles actually reported Jewish hiding places and denounced the Jews as a stain upon the world.

There were also those who refused to harbor them, which was understandable, knowing that such an action could put their own lives at risk.

Finally, though, and most importantly, there were people who risked their own lives to save the Jews, keeping them hidden away from even their own families. Bless these true heroes, many of whom have been honored in the Garden of the Righteous, in Israel.

The Arrival of Hitler's Army in Stanislavov

The German tanks arrived triumphantly in the city of Stanislavov. There was marked unrest among us Jews. How should we behave so that we wouldn't stand out? What could we expect from the occupying forces? We got our answers almost immediately.

Notices were pinned up on trees, posts, and fences around the cities inviting the Jews to a registration process. At the same time, signs appeared prohibiting the entry of Jews and dogs into public parks, cinemas, and theaters.

On the buses and trams, a separate compartment was designated for Jews and dogs, in a clear declaration that, for the Germans, the two breeds—human and animal—were to be considered of equal status.

After a few days, trucks with loudspeakers began to circulate, from which guards ordered Jews to stand outside their homes and hand over any valuable objects, such as Persian rugs, crystal, paintings, silverware, jewelry, and furs.

After complying with this order, we were told that in the coming days we would be taken to a district where we would be among "our own kind" and would work toward the "enlargement of the new homeland."

At first call, we would have to leave our houses with the doors left open behind us, taking only what we could carry.

The Sorting of the Jews

This was how we began our confinement in the poorest district in the city, from which non-Jewish Poles and the Ukrainians were removed and sent to the homes we had previously occupied.

We were herded out of trucks like cattle, into a central square at the beginning of Barewicza Street. Two German officials wasted no time in sitting down behind some desks on which, on one side, was a stack of identity cards, and on the other, was a list of names. With the help of Ukrainians, long lines of men were formed, followed by women in a separate group.

By the side of the square, big trucks waited at the ready, surrounded by Ukrainians waiting to take orders from the "supermen."

Each male Jew presented himself at one of the tables and was looked up and down from head to toe, by a terrible, penetrating gaze, and then, depending on the verdict, received a letter, either *A*, *B* or *C*, to place on his chest.

The letter *A* meant useful for *Arbeit* (work) and was destined only for the young or vigorous adults. The letter *B* indicated people who would be temporarily spared, but who were candidates for the next round of sorting. Finally, the letter *C* was allocated to those who were sick, debilitated, or older, and they were then immediately taken away and thrown into a truck by the Ukrainians.

Uncle Edmund received the letter *A*. Relieved, he returned to the back of the line, along with the women. Uncle Edward was next, and he too received the letter *A*. My stepfather was not so lucky. He was older and had quite a haggard appearance. Also, his posture was affected by the recent development of arthritis in his knee. He received the letter C and was immediately taken away with the other "prizewinners" to wait for a truck.

Mother became desperate, as did Kora, his daughter. Without a second thought, Uncle Edward got back in line, slipping into his pocket the letter A he had just been given. He risked himself for his brother-in-law, and out of love for his sister and my mother, presented himself once again to those murderers. Fortunately he received another letter A, which he pinned to his lapel.

He then ran toward his brother-in-law and simulated picking up an identity card from the floor with the letter A, which he had actually taken from his pocket, and handed it to my stepfather as if he'd lost it. Without waiting for the reaction of the guards, in seeing such daring in a Jew, my fearless uncle quickly tore off the letter C on his brother-in-law's lapel and replaced it with the A. He then led him back to my mother, bringing us joy that is hard to describe, after the shock and desperation we had felt.

Our Miserable Life in the Ghetto

A few days after our transfer to the accommodations chosen for us by the Germans, the women were called up to do forced labor. Mother managed to get work outside the ghetto, sorting the clothing of deported Jews.

At the beginning, we thought that these were clothes left behind by people who could carry no more, but as the days passed, Mother told us that bloodied items had arrived with bullet holes. Faced with the evidence, we were sure "our kind" were being exterminated.

Kora also got a job outside the ghetto, as a housekeeper in Herbert Szpitta's residence. He was a German civilian from Berlin.

My stepfather declared that he was a baker and managed to get a job in the bakery, where the temperature was favorable to the rheumatism that so troubled him.

The bakery made bread for the Germans, but when there was a burnt piece left over, my stepfather would bring it home for me (my being so hungry made it seem delicious) or for Mother to exchange for other foodstuffs, such as flour, tea, and on rare occasions, sugar.

With the constant threat of attack by the Germans, who roamed the city on galloping horses, it was very risky to play on the street, which is why I almost never went out while I was waiting for my family to return. Sometimes I played *queimada* (dodgeball) with other children, which I really enjoyed, but most of the time I stayed at home with my friend Gina, who lived on the same floor.

Our entertainment consisted of games for which we

needed only paper and a pencil. I knew many games that Mother had taught me. In one of them, for example, we would choose a word—preferably a long one—and make as many words as possible using the letters from the main word. Whoever made the most words won the game.

We also had fun skipping and playing hopscotch, hangman, tic-tac-toe, and the alphabet game. Many years later, in Brazil, I played this last game countless times with my children, in the car on the way to São Vicente.

But going back to wartime, as I was saying, most of my day consisted of waiting for Mother to return from her job outside the ghetto and for my stepfather to return from the bakery.

The worst thing was constantly feeling afraid. Hearing shouts, cries, and shots; being alone during German attacks; being subjected to mice, fleas, head lice, insects, and every type of pest—all of this was part of my daily life in that place. That's not to mention the hunger that led me to raking through the trash in search of food.

I even ended up cooking bones that the Germans had thrown to the dogs, as well as liver membranes and grass, which I ate with salt as if it were spinach. If such a vegetable had previously been unpalatable, the hunger that tormented me day and night meant that such food became more than edible.

It was also hunger that drove me, one time, to ignore the danger and pass beneath the wooden fence that surrounded the ghetto to pick potatoes, beetroot, turnips, and leafy vegetables. This was truly reckless, as the wall was under guard and shots could often be heard.

When Mother found out what I had done, she banned me from going back and taking such a risk again. But she herself took risks. Whenever she could, she would hide food under her clothes, such as eggs, a little flour, or sugar.

One time, she wanted to bring me some milk in a small can, but she had to drink it so that she wouldn't be discovered by guards with sniffer dogs.

Nothing could be taken into the ghetto—absolutely nothing. Anybody discovered committing such an infraction would be executed on the spot.

Another time Mother broke the rules was when she dyed a piece of material and a *tallit* (shawl) to make a skirt and blouse for me. This was the way life was—we always needed to be creative to overcome adversities, which were numerous and never-ending.

As residents of the ghetto, we lived apart from the world, which is why we had no idea what was going on, not even what hour, day, or month it was. Our only clues came from Nature.

When the leaves yellowed and began to fall from the trees, we knew that it was the fall. The snow told us that the harsh winter was approaching. The first little flowers emerging through the melting snow were the first signs of spring. And finally the warmer temperatures spoke of summer.

Never-Ending Horrors

As time went on, the German "manhunts" in the ghetto became ever more frequent. They fired many times at random or picked out a victim on a whim.

Another of their abuses was to pull sick people out of the hospital, order them to lie on the grass facedown, and shoot them in the back of the head. Their bodies would lie there for several days like wax figures, with their hospital gowns (which opened at the back) fluttering in the wind, until finally they were taken away by some Jews especially assigned to the task.

Nearly every day I would see handcarts piled high with corpses, one on top of another, being pushed and pulled by hungry Jews, dragging themselves along like the living dead.

The limbs of the bodies shook from the uneven bouncing of the wheels over the cobblestones, so that they seemed to be waving good-bye. These were macabre scenes that I will never be able to forget.

I witnessed many other situations of unimaginable horror, one of which I'm going to relate here. I've never had the courage to tell anyone before now, because it was so degrading.

That I have decided to share this incident now, however reluctantly, is because I think it's important to show the depths of humiliation that humans were driven to by the brutal conditions of the Holocaust.

To continue the story, one day I looked through a window and saw a six- or seven-year-old child vomit on the sidewalk. Soon after, another child of roughly the same age lunged at the remains of the vomit on the sidewalk and ate them, in seeking the food that was systematically denied him because of his only sin: having been born a Jew.

The Jewish Police

The Germans instituted a Jewish police force inside the ghetto to keep order. The Jewish police wore caps with a yellow band, and they carried batons, which they frequently used to punish other Jews, in a show of complicity with the Germans and of subordination that they foolishly thought would help save them.

Shortly before the ghetto was closed down, all those who had been part of the Jewish police were hung from telegraph poles along the main street. And inflicting one more act of mental torture upon us, they made us march past the corpses with our heads up, looking directly at the bodies, which had been swinging from poles for some days. I marched along, frightened to death, fearing one of the bodies would fall down on top of us.

Another Heroic Act
by Uncle Edward

One day, a beautiful young girl was beaten in the street by Streige, a German executioner who would circulate in the ghetto on a huge white horse. On a whim, he gave the girl the chance to save her own life in exchange for her mother's.

Without thinking twice, she entered my grandparents' home at random, pointed at my grandmother Berta, and firmly declared, "this is my mother." The girl was immediately freed, while my grandmother was taken away as the girl's "mother," to join the Jews who would be taken to a "forced labor" camp, which was in fact later identified as an extermination camp.

It did absolutely no good insisting that we'd never even met the girl and begging the guard to understand that she'd acted out the whole scene to save her and her real mother's lives.

My grandfather was desperate, and he began to bang his head against the wall until it was covered in blood. Right then, my uncle Edward arrived. On finding out about this catastrophe, he ran toward the square, where his mother was walking among the other Jews in the direction of the railway station, to wait for the train that would take them away.

The Nazis, high up on their thoroughbred horses, circled the poor victims, who were also under the surveillance of Streige himself and of Krieger, a commander just as cruel as his colleague.

My uncle Filip when he served in the Polish army before the war.

Once again, without missing a beat, Uncle Edward strode up to the horse ridden by Streige with a confident click of his heels and emphatically saluted the "demigod" before addressing him in perfect German: "My name is Edward Blum. I was at the front of the battle between the German army and the Russian troops, taking care of your soldiers wounded in combat, soothing their pain, giving them medicine, treating their wounds as a trained dentist is able. And today, because of a terrible mistake, my mother is being taken away by your soldiers, after being randomly picked out by an unknown youth trying to save her own mother. With all due respect I ask you, General, sir, to spare my poor mother's life, and thus grant justice."

If just talking to a soldier was prohibited, imagine addressing a German official—a powerful "owner" of his prisoners' lives—without being invited. Such a transgression, punishable by death, could have cost my uncle Edward his life in an instant. But miracles can also happen.

Shocked and stupefied by the courage of this young twenty-three-year-old in risking his own life to save his mother's, Streige asked him simply: "What is your mother's name?"

My uncle replied, "Berta Blum," while pointing out my grandmother, who was already waiting in line.

Streige yelled: "Blum, heraus!" (Blum, out!)

My grandmother, still confused by events and without her glasses, couldn't make out her son straightaway, but he ran toward her and they left together, huddled in an embrace.

At home, the family was waiting, desperate for news. When they saw the pair arrive, everyone cried with joy, and I spent many minutes hugging my dear little grandmother, whom I absolutely adored.

Life Hanging by a Thread

Our life constantly hung by a thread, and incidents arose when we least expected them, like the day I went to visit Grandma Berta with my mother.

As my grandma suffered from asthma and cigarette smoke was bad for her, my mother, who had taken up smoking during the war to alleviate her hunger, went to the window so as not to trouble her. At that very moment, Colonel Krieger appeared on his horse, and when he saw Mother smoking (something not permitted for Jews), he ordered the household onto the street. Everyone obeyed except Mother, who was afraid of being shot.

After eyeing each person carefully, Krieger sent a message to Mother: "Warn the woman who stayed inside that this time I'll spare her life, but this had better not happen again". Once again Mother escaped summary execution.

The Fatherless Ones

The day arrived when the Germans chose to eradicate those children who didn't have a father and who, according to the law of the ghetto, couldn't be adopted.

Whenever a "cleansing" operation like this was carried out, the gates were closed and guards were placed at the ready, so that the Jews who worked outside the ghetto couldn't return.

Thus, at sundown, the Germans closed the ghetto and began their persecution of the orphans, entering all of the houses to grab the unfortunate ones who had no father and throw them into trucks or carts to take them away.

In my family, I was the only one with the surname Hitner, from my father. Realizing the danger I was in, I decided to take a small bag that Kora had hidden in the fireplace, which contained trinkets inherited from her mother and which held great sentimental value for her, and I took myself away from the shouts to look for refuge.

In all my relatives' houses, they told me that they would take me in only if I got rid of the bag. They were scared that the Gestapo would mistake this small treasure for jewelry, which would certainly spell death for those involved.

Running around in the middle of the night alone, not knowing what to do, I decided to seek out my "fake uncle," Munio Seibald, the same man who had given us shelter during the invasion by the Russian troops.

He immediately pulled me inside his house, threw Kora's little jewelry bag on top of the closet, and carried me to his daughter Sylwia's bed, covering me with a blanket.

Hours later, the Gestapo knocked on the door. Uncle

Munio showed them his daughter's documents, to prove that there were no fatherless children living there.

In the middle of the night, he woke me and explained that the gates of the ghetto had reopened. It was thus very important that I return home quickly, so my mother would find me there when she arrived. If I wasn't there, she might think that I had been taken away with the other children for termination. And this would have ended her. He was proved absolutely right, as when she saw me, she was so happy that it seemed like I'd been reborn.

The Final Wave

While I was running home, I came across the convoy that was taking away the orphan children. In the middle, I caught a glimpse of my friend Gina, who gave me a good-bye wave.

In the space of a few weeks, her entire family had disappeared, leaving her alone in the world. Her father had been shot, her sister had never returned from work, and her mother had died of starvation.

The death of this dear friend and companion really affected me. Together we had faced the sad days in the ghetto, playing, watching the snow fall from the window, and remembering the time we'd attended the same school, under the Russian rule—a time when, believe it or not, we could even say that we were happier.

Right then, life went on, but with no glimmer of hope for the future.

The Loss of Loved Ones

There was a continuous stream of trucks arriving at the ghetto, piled high with Jewish Hungarians, who were dumped in the Rodolfo Mill, known as Rudolf's Mile. As our building was on the way to the mill, we would see hundreds of hands stretched out asking for food and water each day. Those imprisoned in the mill would shout for help, waving their hands through the windows to attract attention.

On one of these terrible days, my grandfather, who at the time worked in a tannery, arrived home and announced that at night there would be the penultimate round of killing, ahead of the total cleansing of the ghetto. He had come to collect Grandma because, according to information from his director, the tannery would be spared, and the director himself had authorized him to bring someone from his family to stay with him there.

Mother, who was absolutely desperate, asked her father if he'd take me along with Grandma. But the director said that Grandpa would have to choose between taking his wife and taking his granddaughter. On hearing this, Mother dropped the idea.

We said good-bye to my grandparents, not knowing that it would be the last time we'd see them. To this day I can recall the sheer pain of that moment. Having lived with them for so long before the war, I had become so very close to them.

After we bid farewell to my grandparents, Mother and I went straight out to look for another hiding place.

Arriving home (we lived on the ground floor of a three-story building), we saw my stepfather gathered with other residents to decide where we would all hide.

We were aware that the Jews who lived on the third floor had already been taken away to the termination camp. We also knew that there was a small room with a hiding place that would hold up to ten people, behind an enormous closet.

Thus it was quickly decided that women, children, and the elderly would hide there, taking with them water and a minimal amount of food, while the young men would escape to the forest close to the ghetto, after pushing the closet against the wall to conceal the door of the shelter.

In a matter of minutes, I found myself surrounded by several strangers. The majority were women and children, but there were two men, including my stepfather.

We heard the sounds of the closet being pushed and then the young men running out of the building. A few minutes later we heard the gallop of horses and shouts of "Juden, heraus!" (Jews, get out!)

Through a small crack in the roof, my stepfather managed to see a group of Germans and Ukrainians in the middle of the square in front of our building. They were waiting for their colleagues, who had entered the houses to search for victims to drive out, mixing kicks with blows with their rifles.

In our shelter, a couple had brought their exceptional son, an eight-year-old boy called Misio. Out of the blue he stood up and started to repeat, "Já sie nie boje, já sie nie boje." (I'm not afraid.)

My stepfather put his finger on his lips asking for silence, but it did no good. So he asked him, "Misio, do you like chocolate? Remember how tasty it was? If you keep quiet, I'm going to give you a great big piece of chocolate." It was enough to silence Misio.

Soon after, we heard the Germans enter the building

and start banging their rifles on the floors and walls to see if they echoed.

A terrified lady, who was holding two children to her breast, began to sob silently. She said that she lived on the second floor and had left her baby sleeping after feeding him, because there was no way to bring him without compromising our lives. She clung to the hope that the Germans would be quick and her young son would carry on sleeping.

With all the shouts and blows, the baby woke up and started to cry. Then there was a shot, and all went quiet. Realizing what had happened, the child's mother fainted, and she had to be supported by my mother. In this climate of desperation and misery, two women began to tap their chests and murmur a prayer, Shema, Yisrael[10] (Listen, Israel).

Then it was our turn. The "owners of our lives" entered the floor where we were hiding. Seeing the closet that covered the entrance to our hiding place, one of them said, "What do you think? There might be Jews hidden behind here."

The other replied, "Maybe. Let's schieben (pull)."

As there were only two of them, they weren't able to shift the heavy closet. My stepfather, who was sitting on the floor with his back and head against the door, concentrated on pressing hard against it, to prevent even the slightest noise.

Finally, to our immense relief, the German soldiers gave up. This time we ended up owing our lives to a prosaic heavy piece of wooden furniture.

At eight o'clock sharp the next morning, as expected,

_____

10   Shema Yisrael: one of the oldest and most important Jewish prayers, a true declaration of faith.

the Germans left the ghetto, taking their prisoners to their death.

Scared out of our skins, we waited for the younger men to return from the forest to free us. As soon as we left our hiding place, each of us went looking for information about our relatives.

My mother and I visited uncles and cousins who'd survived and, feeling a little calmer, we went off to find my grandparents. We expected them to be at home but found no one. Fearing the worst, we ran toward the tannery.

When we arrived, we asked the watchman about Salo Blum, the Jew who ran the establishment. He informed us that many Jews had been taken away in the trains, and others had returned to their homes.

He then pointed to a pile of documents and ended the conversation by saying that those who had been deported had received instructions to leave their documents behind, because they would no longer be needing them. I saw Mother throw herself at the pile and search desperately for her parents' papers. Tragically, her greatest fears became reality. She found the documents and realized that they had been deported.

I am unable to describe her cry. It was a mixture of deep pain, desperation, impotency, and horror at the tragedy— and also terror at the thought that I could have been taken along with my grandparents. Once more, fate, which had been so cruel to us, spared Mother from suffering something that would have been too much for her to bear.

Mother had a high fever for several days. She became delirious. As we had no analgesics or antipyretics, my stepfather and I would press cold wet cloths to her forehead, pleading to God for her return to normal. The fear of losing her was terrible. She was my whole life. Without Mother, I would have lost all my bearings. I think I would have died of a broken heart.

After some days, the fever subsided, and we immediately prepared to leave the ghetto, before it was razed to the ground. Kora stayed, however, as she was already living at Mr. Szpitta's house, where she worked.

Our Flight from the Ghetto

Between 1942 and 1943, Mother gathered some items of jewelry that she kept in the lining of her coat and used them to buy three birth certificates from a priest. Thus in possession of the documents of three parishioners who had died, we became Polish Catholics.

Under our new identities, I was Eva Rysiek, my mother was Maria Rysiek, and my stepfather was Filip Rysiek.

It was with these documents, one rainy morning, that Mother, my stepfather, and I joined the Jewish train for those who worked outside the ghetto.

As children weren't allowed to leave the ghetto, I clung to my stepfather's waist, hidden under an enormous overcoat that Mother had managed to obtain. I followed in his footsteps but was unable to see anything. We escaped to our lives as fugitives with just the clothes on our backs, some gloves and socks stuffed in the pockets of the overcoat, two sweaters, a face towel on our backs, and our new documents, which would see us through to the end of the war.

A few days later, the Stanislavov ghetto was emptied, and its remaining inhabitants were sent to a concentration camp.

The Fate of My Uncles

Just before the Stanislavov ghetto was emptied, my uncles Edmund and Edward and my aunt Ala all escaped, each to face a different fate.

In Boryslav, Uncle Edmund took up a director's position at a branch of Mr. Herbert Szpitta's scrap yard, under the false name Michal Machnicki. Mr. Szpitta was the German civilian who employed Kora as a housekeeper.

As well as wearing a black stripe on his hat and sleeve, as a fake sign of widowhood, Uncle Edmund pretended that he had a limp, because his documents stated that he had suffered an accident. This disguise was extremely opportune, as it provided a means to escape being called up by the army, while not running the risk of having to strip off for a medical exam.

We knew nothing of Uncle Edward's fate. Only some time later did we discover that he had taken a job in an office. Denounced as a Jew, he was shot in the back while looking out through a window onto the street.

Ala got together with her ex-husband. Due to the clandestine dealings he had with the Germans, hiding flour and sugar for resale, both were arrested. They were both supposed to be released after serving their sentences, but this never happened. Once they were uncovered as Jews, they were executed in the prison courtyard.

We found out what had happened from Hala, my stepfather's sister-in-law, who went to visit Ala, Mother's sister, in prison. Through the window, she asked her what she needed, and my aunt asked for a bar of soap and a toothbrush. Hala returned on the same day to bring her what she had asked for, but it was already too late.

A Vocation Challenged

Hala, who was married to Josef Ringel, my stepfather's eldest brother, survived the war, as did her daughter, Anita Koplewicz, who now lives in Mexico.

Josef was a gynecologist, and he treated the wives of Gestapo members and assisted with childbirth, which is why they promised to spare him. But they didn't keep the promise. He was deported with other Jews to the Janow concentration camp and never returned.

Anita and I.

Anita, on the other hand, was sent to a convent by her mother, where she remained for the duration of the war. When her mother, who was in a terrible state, was finally able to come for her, Anita refused to leave. She said that she wanted to dedicate herself to being a nun, as she felt like Jesus's bride.

None of her mother's appeals could convince her to leave the convent, so Aunt Hala, as I used to call her, asked for help from the resident priest. She told him that she was alone in the world and her daughter was her only reason to live.

So the priest asked to speak to Anita (who had been given the name Cristina at the convent) and told her that Christ wouldn't condone her decision to stay. He promised that if she still felt that this was her vocation one year on, she would be allowed to return and become a nun.

Meanwhile, he made Aunt Hala promise that if her daughter wanted to return to the convent, she would bring her.

Panicking at this possibility, Aunt Hala virtually forced Anita under my wing, asking me to take her to cinemas, theaters, and student parties to make her forget her obsession.

At first when we went out together, she would come against her will, with her head lowered and wearing tightly buttoned dark clothes, her hair in braids.

But gradually she changed. Little by little, Anita stopped talking about the convent, until she never again said that she wanted to go back. Interestingly, after emigrating to Mexico, the former novice nun entered a beauty contest and won first place to become Miss Mexico.

Our Clandestine Life

We spent our first night outside the ghetto at Herbert Szpitta's house. Hiding us away when necessary, he was the "Schindler" of our lives, and he risked his own life numerous times to protect us.

Herbert Szpitta was an elderly German gentleman from Berlin, with no children. His wife lived in Berlin and only visited from time to time.

In Poland, he had taken up the position of general manager of a big company called Amt fuer Apfallstoff Erfasung, where all the scrap metal brought from the branches in Stanislavov, Stryi, and Boryslav was stored.

Szpitta treated Kora as if she were his own daughter, which is why he helped us several times.

Kora's pseudonym was Janina Tanaszczuk. As a precaution, not even Herbert Szpitta's wife knew that Kora was Jewish. When she became suspicious, she questioned her husband, who vehemently denied it.

He also employed a Jewish butler, who took care of the garden and other heavy jobs, such as pumping the frozen water. This entailed first pouring a bucket of hot water into the pump and then using all his might to force the water into the kitchen. He also used to take care of the shopping for the house and shined Mr. Szpitta's boots. He had been born Luis Karliner (Lipa), but his false Ukrainian name was Oleksa Sorokoput ("Olek").

On Sundays, the day of rest, Kora and Lipa would go out for the day or go to the cinema. Over time, they fell in love, and soon after the end of the war, they married.

But returning to our only night at Mr. Szpitta's house, it was decided that Mother and I would travel to Stryi, the city where the main branch of the scrap metal company was located and the main residence of our benefactor.

We stayed at Mr. Szpitta's home in Stryi for a few days, but as we had nowhere to go, we went to the ghetto in the city, which hadn't yet been pulled down. Incredible as it may seem, we felt safer among our own people, despite their being condemned.

The rulers of the ghetto were a Mr. Zauerbrun and a famous pediatrician and distant relative of my stepfather, Dr. Huterer, who used to travel with the family to the Brzuska farm to take part in the hunts before the war.

Before leaving for Stryi, we traveled by train to Kraków to meet a couple, some friends who had spent some vacations in Brzuska. She, Lusia Koczynska, was Jewish, and he, Wladek Koczynski, was a Christian.

We were surprised to learn that Lusia had separated from Wladek, who had left her after falling in love with his partner's wife. Lusia explained that it would be very difficult for us to stay for very long, because every Saturday she hosted wine-soaked evenings for German officials, which continued into the early hours.

Even so, we hid in a room some distance from where the "guests" would be housed. We intended to stay until we managed to find a safe place to rent, but we changed our minds after hearing the rowdy reveling of the drunken guests so close by.

So we decided to seek out Wladek, who welcomed us into his workplace, a car body shop, but he told us that, regrettably, his current wife would never agree to hide Jews. He told us we could stay for the night in one of the cars, and he also brought us a snack, but he asked us to leave early the next morning before the mechanics arrived.

Early the next morning, we left to look for somewhere else to stay, before heading back to the city where my stepfather was.

Confiscated Document

We managed to find a guesthouse that had a single room where several people lived. The owner, very taken aback at Mother's distinguished appearance, offered us a bed in a room with the other guests, but in a separate space partitioned by a curtain.

The houseguests included a couple who put on street shows in the city squares. A famous trick of theirs involved a woman lying in a closed box, through which her male companion plunged several swords. At the end, the woman would leave the box, unharmed and smiling, acknowledging the applause and collecting money from the audience. I was fascinated by this show, particularly as I was privileged to be the only witness to the rehearsals.

Another character was a mysterious gentleman who would leave every morning wearing a smoking jacket and return only at the end of the afternoon. He would take great care with his appearance, smoothing down his middle partg with plenty of brilliantine and keeping his vast mustache strictly in check with black tape and elastic.

After a fruitless few days searching for a safer place to live, we decided to stay one last night and then leave the next morning.

We were just going to sleep when there were some loud knocks on the door. Shortly afterward, some German policemen entered to examine the documents of all the guests. They ordered everyone to get dressed and wait in the corridor, because we were all to be taken to a Polish labor camp.

Behind the curtain, frozen with fear, Mother and I waited to see what would happen. We were hoping we wouldn't be discovered. Unfortunately, one of the Germans pulled back the curtain and asked us for our documents, questioning why we were there.

Mother explained that she had come to Kraków because she was sick and was going to start treatment. She produced the doctor's certificate, which had been duly stamped and proved her claim.

They picked out the only one of my mother's documents in which the name and surname had been altered. It was one of the documents we had purchased that had belonged to the deceased Christians. The surname Ringel had been scratched off and Rysiek written in its place, a forgery that was easily spotted under a light.

He stared at Mother, comparing her to the photograph, and said that he would take the document away to the Gestapo, where it could be retrieved the next day. And then he left, taking the other residents with him.

Trip to the Gestapo

Early the next morning, Mother woke me saying she hadn't slept the whole night, worrying about what to do, because there was no way we could travel without her document. It was common knowledge that only very rarely did anyone leave the Gestapo headquarters alive.

We paid for our accommodations, bid farewell to the owner of the guesthouse, thanking her for everything, and set off in the direction of the Gestapo building, carrying an enormous suitcase.

Almost directly in front of the building, we found a church with many steps leading up to it. Mother climbed half the steps, put down the case, and told me, "Sweetheart, wait here for me for one hour. If I haven't returned by then, promise me that you'll go and find a convent somewhere. Tell them you're an orphan and ask them for shelter to save yourself."

After many hugs and kisses, she walked away. In the distance I saw her ring the bell on the front door of the Gestapo building. It opened, and she was beckoned in. I waited, listening to the clock tower sounding out the longest minutes of my life. When half an hour had passed, I left the heavy bag on the step and ran into the church, crying, praying, and pleading with God to bring my mother back to me.

I returned to the step and sat on top of the case, waiting anxiously with my eyes fixed on the Gestapo building door. After a further wait, although I couldn't say how long, Mother appeared, tired but delighted. She came running to meet me.

We sped off to the railway station and took a train to

Stryi. On the way, Mother told me what had happened. After wandering along several corridors and going up many stairs, she came across a guard who directed her to the commander. She introduced herself, saying that she had come to collect a document that had been confiscated the previous day by the police. The commander pointed to a small table that was littered with papers collected from people who'd been arrested. He invited her to pick hers out.

She searched through the papers feverishly, trying not to appear nervous. She found her document and handed it to the official. He walked to the window, took a look at the photograph, and quickly returned the paper, without holding it up to the light.

The commander warned her that the place where the document had been seized wasn't safe and that she was lucky not to have been deported with all the others. Mother thanked him, needing to really control herself to keep from flying along the corridors and down the stairs to meet me.

Accused of Espionage

We arrived in Stryi and wandered aimlessly before stumbling upon a convent. We knocked on the gate, and a nun peered out at us through a hatch. We begged her to let us spend the night. Fortunately, when she saw a lady with a little girl, she took pity on us and gave us shelter, feeding us with tea and bread.

Early the next morning, we thanked her for her hospitality and left to search for a place to rent once again. Mr. Szpitta would then bring my stepfather to join us.

Unfortunately, we were arrested by a Ukrainian soldier, who suspected that we were Polish spies, plotting against the Nazis.

The soldier said that we'd been seen delivering an envelope when we arrived at the railway station. I was two paces away from Mother, and she motioned for me to keep back. The soldier asked who I was, and Mother replied that I'd just been giving her some information, because she was new to the city. To give credence to this idea, she turned to me and said, "You can go, little girl. Thank you. I don't need you anymore."

But go where? I continued to follow her from a distance, hiding behind some posts as I went. When I realized that the soldier was leading her to the Ukrainian police station, I didn't hesitate, crying out, "Mom, don't leave me!"

The soldier turned and shouted back, "Ah, so she's your mother? In that case, you can come too!"

We were placed in separate rooms. After hours of worry, I saw two soldiers carrying a bucket of water and a thick rope. I asked them what they were going to do with them, and they replied, "If your mother doesn't confess that you are spies, we will start to hang her. And if she faints, we'll throw the water on her."

Hearing this, I didn't stop to think and just screamed out, "Don't do this, for the love of God! I confess. Yes, we are spies!"

As a result of my act of desperation, we were escorted to the Polish police station. My mother couldn't believe what I'd done and said resignedly, "Ritusia, you've buried us."

At the time, still in shock, all I managed to say was, "But they said they were going to hang you ..."

Escorted by two Ukrainians, we arrived at the police station.

After confiscating our documents, they left us in a cell that looked like a cellar, because it was well belowground. The floor and walls were covered in small stones, and there was a small lamp hanging from the ceiling. After a few minutes, the commander came along with two old blankets, which he handed to us to lay on the floor and keep us warm. I fell asleep quickly, but occasionally when I opened my eyes, I would see Mother watching over me and keeping away the mice, which were all over the place.

Later still, the commander appeared again with a drink to warm us. When he entered the cell, on both occasions, I noticed him looking at Mother's hand, on which she wore a small diamond ring. The jewel proved that she really was a Polish Catholic, as Jews were not permitted any type of accessory.

Mother also noticed the commander's interest and offered him the jewel, saying, "Commander, sir, please take this ring for your wife and leave the door open for us to escape. If not for me, then for this girl who has her whole life in front of her."

"I can't do that," he replied. "I would be risking my own life." He left in a hurry and didn't return.

Early the next morning, we heard a noise. Mother climbed up on a pile of bricks to take a look at what was going on through a small crack in the wall. She spotted a Jew wearing an armband with a Star of David, who was crouching down pumping up bicycle tires.

When she called to him, he became afraid, but Mother calmed him. "I'm Jewish too. Please run to the ghetto and tell the presidents, Mr. Zauerbrun and Dr. Huterer, that Nusia Ringel is under arrest in these police cells."

After several hours, we were called into the commander's office. He returned the documents to Mother and told us that we were free to go because of lack of evidence. Mother was even brave enough to ask him for advice. "Sir, do you think I should return to the ghetto or try to go underground?"

With his attention divided between her and her photo on the document, he considered for a moment. "In your place, and with your appearance, I would try to live outside the ghetto, because it will be eradicated very soon."

A New Residence

With nowhere to go, we returned straight to the ghetto, where we found out that our freedom was not due to lack of evidence, but to the initiative of the two presidents who knew our family. They had gathered large sums of money to buy the silence of the Ukrainian and Polish police chiefs.

After a few days in Stryi, we were reunited with a family we had met in the Stanislavov ghetto, the Zaifman couple and their son. The wife was called Fani, and their eight-year old son, Tolek. I can't quite remember her husband's first name.

The couple sought out my mother with a proposal: "We know that you don't have the financial means to leave the ghetto, but your daughter's and your Aryan looks might prove useful to us. If you were to rent a small house on the outskirts of the city in your name, at our expense, you would be able to move freely around the city doing your shopping and living a normal life. Your husband and the three of us, who all look like Semites, could hide away and not leave the house. In return, we would pay for all the food."

We had no choice but to accept. Rumors abounded that the ghetto would be razed, and having no savings to our name, we wouldn't be able to survive alone. We agreed.

The next day, Mother managed to sneak out of the ghetto to look for a house. She found one that would accommodate two families and was a little isolated from the other houses in the town.

The house contained old furniture, including a large closet, three single beds, a table, and four chairs. The floor under the table was covered by a small rug, which concealed the opening to an unventilated pantry, used to keep potatoes, carrots, and beetroot during the winter.

And this was how the new phase of our lives began. At first, everything seemed to be fine. Mother made a few friends among the neighbors and justified her reserved lifestyle and lack of visitors by saying that her husband was an official in the Polish army, waging war at the battlefront.

Gestapo Once Again

One day, a neighbor made an unexpected visit to warn Mother that a Ukrainian soldier was entering all the houses on the street asking for Maria Rysiek. He said that she was under suspicion because she had been buying a lot of food, despite living alone with only one daughter.

Mother thanked the neighbor and entered the house. She told my stepfather and Mr. Zaifman to hide behind the closet and hastily dragged away the table, lifted up the carpet, and crept into the pantry, which wasn't big enough for someone to sit down or stand up, so she had to lie on top of the potatoes.

We'd barely had time to replace the carpet and arrange the furniture on top, when we heard loud knocks on the door. I went to answer without rushing, so that Fani and Tolek were able to start playing dominoes. My heart was racing. I knew that Mother wouldn't be able to stay in that cubicle for very long without any ventilation.

When the soldier asked for her, we told him that she'd had to travel. Ignoring the reply, he sat on a chair, a sarcastic expression on his face, and said that he had all the time in the world to wait for her. Time virtually stood still.

The men behind the closet held their breath. Fani carried on playing dominoes. And I was absolutely desperate with the thought that Mother might suffocate.

Unable to control myself any longer, I heaved the table away without another thought, lifted up the carpet with Tolek's help, and opened the trapdoor. Mother climbed out, half-suffocated, coughing hard, and breathless. Fani shot me an indignant look. The soldier exclaimed, "I knew it! The four of you are coming with me to the Gestapo right now. And you can take just one bag each."

In the middle of that terrible scene, I still remembered to grab a pair of warm slippers that my grandfather had made especially for my mother before the war, because she had always felt the cold in her feet.

The men who had hidden behind the closet managed to escape in the middle of the night to the Stryi ghetto, the only place where a Jew could find shelter.

Fani and her son were taken to prison and put in a cell for Jews, because there was no denying their Semitic origins, as the son had been circumcised.

Mother and I were interrogated by the Gestapo, accused of harboring Jews, and we were led into a room with a small bed pushed against the wall. Four *Obersturmbannführer* (SS colonels) waited in each corner.

One of them was holding a whip and ordered Mother to undress and lie facedown on the bed. She did as she was told and stripped to her underclothes. As she was about to lie down, an older, graying official appeared and shouted at the young torturers, "What's happening here?" Turning to Mother, he ordered her to get dressed and go to another room, where the interrogation began.

They asked her why she hid Jews knowing that it was punishable by death. Mother, as always, justified herself by saying that as she wasn't a communist, she had been arrested several times by the NKWD during the Russian occupation and had received help from these Jews. Also, she explained, she had no money to feed her daughter and believed that being shot was not as cruel as dying of starvation.

The Germans were still unconvinced and continued their questions to see if she would contradict herself and reveal that she was Jewish. But she was able to stay strong.

Still doubtful, they resorted to puerile tests. First they gave her a plate with some pasta and sauce to eat, because the Germans apparently believed the Jews had a habit of first eating the pasta and then the sauce.

Next, they told her to strike a match, believing that the "cowardly" Jews struck matches from the inside out, while "fearless" Aryans did the opposite. Mother was already aware of these absurd beliefs, so she was able to pass both tests.

Next, a German began looking at photos of Brzuska, which Mother had carelessly brought with her. After each photo showing her in a riding habit, boots, and leather jacket, he would repeat, "You were a very pretty Jew," and Mother, in turn, would correct him, repeating, "Catholic."

Faced with a lack of evidence, they attempted one final test: they took some blood samples to be analyzed in a laboratory in Berlin, because the Polish laboratories were not trusted, in the hope that traces of Semitic origins would be found.

After about two days, the results arrived. To our immense relief it had been decided that our blood was Aryan, and we therefore were deemed worthy to live among the "pure" German race.

While waiting for the results, Mother tried every means she could to keep me calm. She explained that this type of exam was pathetic and there was no difference at all between Aryan blood and that of any other race, whether black, yellow, or red—all blood was the same. But I thought that anything could happen among all the madness and our forged documents, and I was frightened to death.

After all this torment and lack of evidence, they sent us to the same prison where Fani and Tolek had been taken. But we were thrown into a cell occupied just by

Christians. Among our cell mates were several prostitutes playing indecent jokes on each other—which prompted Mother to cover my eyes—a woman who had murdered her stepfather, and a female thief. Mother and I, the heavyweight "criminals," made up the final members of the cell.

Elegance in Check

To lighten a little the memory of the sad facts that follow, I'd like to relate a funny episode that we witnessed, which shows how human beings are capable of forgetting their misfortune for a few moments, even under the most desperate of circumstances.

It all began when the cell door opened and in walked an elegantly dressed lady, replete with fur coat and hat, gloves, and beautiful, shiny high-heeled boots. From each finger hung little packages, wrapped in fine ribbon.

She caused us all to fall silent, before Mother whispered in my ear, "This lady must be a representative of the Red Cross, which sometimes brings food for prisoners."

The lady studied her surroundings, and then someone pushed a small stool toward her so she could sit. She began to tell her story. "My dear ladies, my name is Katarzyna. I've been working in the department that restocks the flour for the army and, for the first time, I hid half a kilo away to take home. And I was caught and sent to this prison. Can you believe the injustice, ladies! I have brought some sandwiches that I can share with you all. But before I do, could you please direct me to the bathroom."

Someone pointed to a barrel beside the wall, which was so high that whoever wanted to use it would need a stool just to climb up to it. The lady looked incredulous and asked if we were joking. When we said no, she huffed indignantly, "Á co to to nie!" (Ah, spare me this, please!). Not half an hour later, this distinguished lady was sitting up on the barrel, hat and all. Before nightfall she was released, and she left her packets of sandwiches with us.

Face-to-Face with Death

After a week, during which Mother and I had been interrogated on a daily basis while many of the prisoners from our cell had been released, we were informed that all of the prisoners from all of the cells—except for the Jews—should stand in front of the patio wall, where they would be shot.

My mother when she left prison.

Mother hugged me with all her might. For the first time I could see that she was absolutely terrified, because she realized that there was no escape. This time, it was my turn to try to calm her: "Mother, this won't hurt a bit. It'll be just a 'prick'—like an injection—and it'll be over. We are going to meet up with everyone we love."

With this thought in mind, we stepped out to meet our fate, trembling uncontrollably. When everyone was in front of the wall, which stretched a long way, the official decided, on a pure whim, that every tenth person would be saved. And with his gun pointed toward us, he started to count out calmly, "One, two, three, four, five, six, seven, eight, nine ... ten, heraus!" (out!).

Miraculously, the impossible happened: not only were "we" the tenth person, but also—inexplicably—we were counted as just one person, perhaps because we were hugging each other so hard. And this was how, once again, Mother and I escaped certain death.

Assumed Identity

One day, the guards announced to everyone that the president of the ghetto would come to take away the Jewish prisoners to do forced labor. They opened up all of the cells, and the prisoners filed out into the corridor.

Dr. Huterer was taking down the names of the prisoners he would take with him, while the dogs barked fiercely. Realizing that this would be the only chance to escape from prison, Mother pushed through the crowd. Ignoring the vehement protests from the Germans, who cried out, "You're not Jewish, so you're not allowed to speak with the Jew," she said in a low voice, "Sir, do you remember me? I am Nusia Ringel, from Brzuska. Please take me with you, sir."

With his eyes trained on his notepad, where he was scribbling down names, he whispered quickly, "Ma'am, you must state that you are Jewish, as it's the only way I'll be able to take you. I have absolutely no power over the Christian prisoners."

With no time to waste, Mother grabbed my hand and announced to the world, "We are Jewish!"

Her emphatic declaration triggered plenty of commotion among the German guards, who were convinced that we weren't Jews. They barely managed to keep hold of their dogs, which snarled fiercely and barked nonstop, ready to attack us.

Finally under Dr. Huterer's escort, we returned to the ghetto and were immediately disinfected from the head lice that had camped in our hair and the seams of our clothes, biting us incessantly. We wasted no time in planning our escape, as we knew that the whole place was due to be razed.

While there, we discovered that Tolek, the son of the Zaifman couple, had been killed while he was alone with his father. After this, Mr. Zaifman and his wife had left the ghetto to find a different hiding place.

After a time in the ghetto, under the shadow of its impending liquidation, we had no option but to escape, leaving my stepfather behind at Mr. Herbert Szpitta's house for a few nights[11]. As soon as we were able to find refuge, we hoped to return for him.

We boarded a train to Boryslav, to meet up with my uncle Edmund Blum, now known as Michal Machnicki, who managed one of Mr. Szpitta's scrap yards.

Uncle Edmund.

---

11   During the War, Jewish men had to be particularly careful, given they were circumcised and therefore easily identified as Jews, even with fake papers.

Life in Boryslav

We rang the bell at the company's front gate. Uncle Edmund, who both worked and lived at the company, put his head in his hands when he saw us. "What are you doing here?" he asked, gravely concerned. After we told him of our adventures, he hid us away in an attic, which had a chimney in the middle of the room, until we found alternative shelter.

The room had been invaded by bugs. At night, they crept out from between the cracks in the walls *en masse*. But Mother, ever the warrior, burned them with a candle to protect me from their bites.

A few weeks passed. We remained there in complete silence, so as not to put Uncle Edmund or ourselves at risk. Mother finally managed to find a house with two bedrooms, one of which was already occupied. However, the house had separate entrances.

Given this development, Mr. Szpitta thought the time had arrived to bring my stepfather from Stryi, where he'd been hiding for some weeks. One night, he placed a Bavarian hat on my stepfather's head and a swastika on his lapel. He suggested that my stepfather travel in the carriage reserved for Germans, and that he cover his face with a German newspaper and pretend to be asleep until the end of the journey. Should he be uncovered, he was to deny knowing Szpitta or having any connection with him whatsoever.

Fortunately, they arrived without incident and, in the black of night, my stepfather slipped into the house. From this point on, we began to whisper so that a man's voice wouldn't be heard coming from the house.

During the day, my stepfather would remain seated behind the closet, relying on a bucket with a lid for his personal needs. This was emptied into a cesspit behind the house when it got dark. When he needed to cough, the two of us coughed together to disguise the noise. Only at night was he finally able to come out from behind the closet to wash and sleep.

Mother took on the position of her brother's secretary. To keep up appearances, she addressed him as "sir" while he called her, "ma'am." She would leave the house in the morning and return only at the end of the afternoon. Meanwhile, I kept myself busy by cleaning our house, cooking, and washing clothes. And in the backyard, I planted a few vegetables—carrots, potatoes, parsley, spring onions, radishes, and lettuce—using seeds that a neighbor gave me.

Our Bunker "Tenants"

In Boryslav at the scrap metal yard overseen by Uncle Edmund, the Jews brought in sections of track, cisterns, and other items in wheelbarrows.

One day while my uncle was inspecting a delivery, a Jewish couple approached him. The man spoke to him reluctantly. "Dear Mr. Machnicki, forgive me for addressing you this way. I know that it isn't allowed for Jews to approach Aryans, but this could be in your interest. Your kindly appearance has given us the courage to make you a proposal. We were the former owners of this house that now serves as a scrap metal yard. Before the Germans invaded Poland, we decided to build a bunker underneath this rabbit hutch to protect us from Russian bombing. We have seen that you, your secretary, and daughter are going through hard times. We have money, so allow us to use the hiding place I mentioned, and in exchange, we will keep you in food until the end of the war. There are eight of us—the Tannenbaum couple, their son Poldek and his fiancée Lusia, Anda Katz, Binka Kulawicz, and Mrs. Aizenstein and her daughter."

My uncle promised to think about it. After talking it over with Mother, they decided to accept the offer, knowing that should the eight be discovered, it would mean certain death for us all. But we had no option, as we barely had money for food. This was also about saving lives. On the night we had agreed upon, the group split into pairs, and everyone went down to the bunker.

To avoid suspicion, Mother would buy our food, such as flour, sugar, rice, beans, and beverages, from different establishments. Afterward, everything was fed down a pipe into the bunker.

One time, I was carrying some bread that I'd disguised by hiding it under some grass, to make it look like food for the rabbits. A German policeman stopped me and asked me what I had in the bag. I showed him its contents, making every effort to control my trembling hands. He lifted some of the grass but soon let me go. Fortunately, the bread was well hidden underneath.

On Sundays, when the company gates were closed, our "tenants" would finally be able to bathe, wash clothes, bask in a little sun, and take the opportunity to stock the bunker with some different foods, such as beef and horse meat, poultry, fat, and some fruits and vegetables, which couldn't be fed through the pipe during the week.

A Whistleblower's "Reward"

At this time, Mr. Aizenstein, who was director of the ghetto in Boryslav, decided to move his wife and daughter from the bunker where we were hiding them, because he felt it was unsafe there.

Following the closure of the ghetto that he ran, the Gestapo promised him a travel permit if he located and handed over twenty Jewish families.

This man searched the city door to door, accompanied by police and their fierce dogs. He also explored the forest and opened up clearings, trying to find his victims.

Aware of this insane manhunt, Mother and my uncle Edmund couldn't relax for a minute, because they realized that Aizenstein knew of the hiding place where his own wife and daughter had been sheltered. The only thing he didn't know was that we were also Jews.

When she passed him on the street, Mother would look away, afraid that he would denounce her for hiding Jews and use the residents of the bunker to add to the total of condemned that he needed to reach his target. But he didn't blow the whistle on us.

In the end, he was able to round up the twenty families that the Gestapo required of him. He handed them over at the railway station, where the train was waiting that would take them to their death. But then the Germans pushed him inside too, shouting, "Now that you have handed over the twenty families, you can join them and make one more." As for his wife and daughter, we never heard what happened to them.

Conversion to Catholicism

Every Sunday I would go to mass, sometimes accompanied by Mother, to prove that we were Christians. Once per month, I would also go to confession and take communion. This routine repeated itself rigidly, month after month, until one day the local priest, Lancki, called me into the sacristy and said, "I have come to realize that you are an exemplary Catholic, who always comes to confession, takes communion, and never misses mass. But despite all of this, I believe that you aren't really a Catholic, but a Jew. I don't convert anyone for money—I only believe in saving souls. So, if your family agrees, come along to my parish tonight, and I will marry your parents and baptize and confirm you all."

When I arrived home, I spoke to my mother and stepfather, who thought Father Lancki's idea was a good one. When night fell, the three of us left for the church, where the priest and two witnesses (his housekeeper and a sacristan) awaited.

For the conversion, we used our true names, to which was added a new baptismal name. Mother chose Teresa and I, Krystyna. My stepfather was the only one who kept his birth name.

The conversion certificates, with our real names, could not be used during the occupation, because the Germans considered people Jews until three generations had passed since conversion, but they were extremely useful when we requested our visas for entry into Brazil. But I'm getting ahead of myself.

My conversion certificate.

Jews would pay huge sums of money to people who processed the identity paper used by the Third Reich, called *Kennkarte*. However, not all would take the risk. Mother courageously took the risk herself, went to the Gestapo and managed to get this fingerprinted document, with which she was able to move around the streets of the city.

Without the Kennkarte, the chance of survival was small.

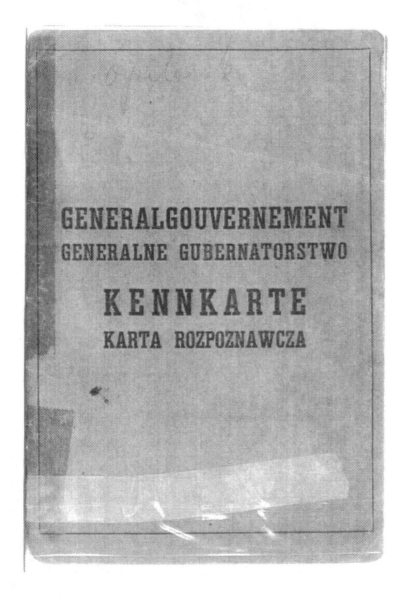

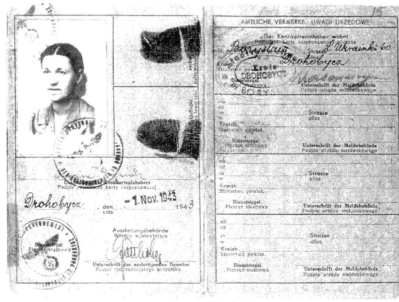

138

Uncontrollable Panic

One day, I went out to buy some bread when some Polish boys ran up behind me and started shouting, "Jew, Jew." Panic-stricken, I flew to the gate of our house and ran inside. The boys kept on shouting, "There is a Jewish girl hidden here!"

Mother gathered her courage, went outside, and said in an authoritative voice, "What do you mean, Jew?! A German official lives here, and if you don't get out of here quickly, he'll be out in a flash to grab you all." Frightened, they all ran off.

After this incident, I would leave the house only at the end of the day when it was already dark, and even then, I would run rather than walk.

My panic at that time was such that my facial expression would give me away, because I looked so scared. To combat this, when I had a bad toothache and needed to go to the dentist, Mother bandaged my face, leaving just one eye uncovered for me to see, so that I wouldn't raise suspicion among the locals.

Living with the Enemy

When, by order of the Gestapo, the people were forced to make a room available for officials, Mother was obliged to take my stepfather out into the suburbs at night, to a hut where Stefa lived.

A country-dweller, Stefa was quite friendly with Mother and agreed to hide my stepfather after she was given a milking cow by one of Mother's acquaintances, a German civilian who was leaving Poland. Stefa promised to feed my stepfather and provide him with a liter of fresh milk every day.

Thus, when Colonel Herbert Kranz arrived with his belongings, the room that my stepfather had occupied was free and bore no trace of him.

Even though she dressed modestly, Mother's beauty always shone through, even when she was wearing a head scarf or cap.

During the war, she passed herself off as the wife of a Polish captain who had not yet returned from the battlefront, yet she still received several romantic approaches and even marriage proposals. But she made it clear to all her potential suitors that she would continue to wait for her husband. Any relationship, therefore, was destined to remain at a platonic level.

She was held very dear by the neighbors, whom she treated with respect and as equals, even the most humble, such as builders, blacksmiths, teamsters, and cleaners.

As for Colonel Herbert Kranz, he also fell for *Frau* Maria, even though there was never any romance between them. He would bring us ham, meat, and biscuits from his quarters. He was hooked on Mother, and I realized that she was also attracted to this handsome, fascinating man, although she would never allow herself the slightest gesture that might reveal this to him.

I believe that his treating her with respect and holding her in great esteem contributed to her feelings. We never spoke a word about this, but she thought it funny that when Kranz was at home I would never leave her side, as if I needed to look out for her on behalf of my stepfather. After all, I thought it was my duty to take care of my mother and protect her in every sense of the word.

Several times while the two of them talked in the kitchen late into the night, I would stay awake even though I could hardly keep my eyes open, and I allowed myself to sleep only after Kranz had finally gone.

New Tenants

Some months before the German withdrawal, there was a knock at the door, and there before us were the Zaifman couple, who had been ejected from their previous hiding place due to a lack of money.

We never discovered how they found us. They had come to ask Mother to hide them, because they had nowhere else to go. Mother explained that there was no room, but even so, she asked them to wait for a few hours to see what she could do.

My mother went to see her "brother boss" and told him everything about the couple. And this was how they ended up occupying a bunker smaller than the one that Uncle Edmund had discovered, close to the rabbit cage. After the war, the couple went to Israel, where they had another child. A long time later, we found out that Mr. Zaifman had died of a heart attack while sitting in a barber's chair.

Kranz, Heraus (Out)

When finally—to our great joy—the Germans began their withdrawal, it was also time for Herbert Kranz to leave. As he said good-bye to Mother, he declared that he would return to marry her if her husband didn't return from the battlefront (the husband that she had invented, remember). He asked her to keep herself as beautiful as she was, suggesting that her few strands of gray hair only enhanced her beauty.

After he had made his exit, we realized that he had forgotten his monogrammed velvet case, in which he kept his shaving accessories and his brush and polish to keep his boots permanently shined.

The last thing we wanted was for Mother's admirer to have a pretext to come back, so I went running after him. He had already mounted his black horse, ready to lead the march of his platoon of soldiers. In double-quick time, I jumped up to reach his hand and hand him his case.

This simple act caused us a future headache—as soon as the Russians returned, I was accused of running after a German official to say good-bye, and worse still, of handing him a gift. Many exhausting hours were needed to convince our interrogators of what really happened ...

A Friendship Miraculously Recovered

After the return of the Russian forces, the Jews were released from the bunker below the rabbit hutch. At this time I got to know Binka Kulawicz, a girl who was part of that group.

To her, I wasn't Jewish. Even so, a friendship formed between us that was as strong as it was brief. Before we went our separate ways, she wrote a poem in my diary, which I have kept to this day.

Sixty years later, at the beginning of 2007, I received an e-mail from a teacher, Father Tadeusz Wrobel of Warsaw, telling me that he was writing a book about Jews from the city of Boryslav. During his research, he discovered that I had lived there, and he asked me to describe to him everything that I and my family had been through back then.

I corresponded with him over a number of weeks, answering questions and providing details. Among all the things I wrote, I described how Mother, Uncle Edmund, and I—who at the time used false names—had hidden Jews beneath the hutch where we bred rabbits.

Sometime later, I received a letter from Sabina van der Linden, telling me that she had heard of me through Father Wrobel, whom she also had contacted. Just like me, she had related that she had been saved by Michal Machnicki, Maria Rysiek, and her daughter, Eva Rysiek, who accommodated her in a bunker below a rabbit hutch. When he connected the different sources of information, Father Wrobel became sure that I was part of the family who had helped to save her, and he immediately gave her my address.

The sheer emotion that I experienced on receiving this news was indescribable. Words cannot express what we felt the first time we wrote each other. From this moment, Binka's (Sabina's) only wish was to meet me so that we could share a strong embrace. And, happily, this actually came to pass.

Binka and her husband, Kjeld, flew all the way from Sydney, where they live, to São Paulo just to see me. The few days we spent together were hardly sufficient to reminisce about all the common experiences we had shared. We spent the whole time together, speaking in Polish about our lives. Only the curiosity of one of my children or grandchildren could interrupt our conversation, albeit for only a few moments.

Finally, what had been unimaginable had happened after such a long time, even though we had had no contact and no indication that we both had survived. And it was here in Brazil, so far from our roots, that we were reunited. Even now, I feel the tug of the emotions I felt at that time.

Binka (Sabina van Lieden) and her husband, Kjeld.

In 2005, Sabina van der Linden was chosen to represent all of the Holocaust survivors worldwide, during the inauguration of the Holocaust Memorial in Berlin. During her speech, she drew tears from the audience when she said that hers was the voice of "six million murdered Jews and their survivors."

The Second Russian Arrival

During the period between the Germans' withdrawal and the Russians' arrival in the city, we were left completely destitute. The German mark no longer had any value, and the Russian ruble was not yet in circulation.

These were difficult days. To survive, we were forced to trade. I remember, for example, picking pears from the tree in our backyard with a colleague of mine and then exchanging them for bread, milk, or potatoes.

With the return of the Russians, we were able to sell our "produce" for rubles, the currency brought in by the new "owners" of Poland.

With her eye for an opportunity, Mother quickly learned how to make vodka, and with the help of her neighbor, she spent whole nights distilling the product, using improvised tubes.

As the Russian authorities prohibited any type of activity that generated a profit, she had to make sure she kept the whole process underground.

When Russian soldiers were anonymously tipped off, they invaded our house in search of material produced by "comrade" Maria. Mother lost no time in going to a small storage cupboard where she kept boxes of candles to sell in a neighboring city and getting rid of the packaging. She threw the boxes out the window, so that when the soldiers entered they found nothing.

A Short "Time-Out"

Mother in 1945.

Today is March 8, International Women's Day. I cannot think of a more appropriate date to pay tribute to the most courageous, admirable, intelligent, happy, and beautiful fighter of a woman whom I have ever known—my mother.

As well as saving my life countless times, covering me with her own body to protect me from bombs, rats, and the cold, she was a model of strength and solidarity in helping to save the lives of many others.

For me, it was a great joy, and I was so lucky to be her daughter! When she passed away, she left us with a very special legacy of love, heroism, courage, and ethics.

Back to Katowice

After some time, the Russian authorities declared that Polish citizens would be able to return to their cities of origin, and they allocated some freight cars on trains to transport us.

After a long journey, we arrived in Katowice. We found out that our apartment was occupied by Dr. Hoff, an attorney colleague of my uncle. We could have asked him to leave, but we didn't, as he had been a friend before the war.

The authorities assigned an apartment for us, in the vicinity of the old one, which also had five bedrooms, two furnished living rooms, and a grand piano, similar to the one we had had previously.

With the war over, the survivors went looking for their relatives in the hope of finding them alive. To help in this search, long lists with the names of those missing were fixed to the walls of some of the buildings in Katowice and other cities. I went to look for my father's name and those of other relatives on a daily basis—always in vain.

Through a survivor of a concentration camp in Janow, we came to hear that, before being deported, Father had taken Oscar, my little seven-month-old half brother, to a Christian couple he was friends with. They promptly agreed to hide him and return him after the war, if Father survived. If he didn't, they would adopt Oscar as their son.

Everything was arranged until the moment when the boy's diaper needed changing and the wife discovered that he had been circumcised. The fear of being reported by neighbors for hiding a Jew made her return little Oscar. Perhaps his fate was that of many other children—to be tied up in a sack and thrown alive into an enormous crater, and covered with earth, while the little bodies still wriggled with the remainder of life.

To save time, other children were barbarically torn from their mothers' clutches by the Germans and speared on the sharp iron railings that surrounded the houses.

As for Father, we were told that he contracted typhus in the concentration camp. So that he wouldn't infect the other prisoners, he was thrown against an electric fence, thus avoiding the need to waste ammunition in killing him.

On this day, the tremendous hope that I had nurtured of being reunited with him was torn away from me, but what remained was the love and admiration I always felt for him, which will stay with me for the rest of my days.

Part Three:
After The War

The New Beginning

Broken and tormented by the memories of our recent past, we began our lives again in 1945. My uncle reassumed his original surname and placed a sign on the door of the building: "Edmund Blum—Attorney."

My mother and stepfather, fearful of the anti-Semitic protests that persisted, decided to continue using their false documents.

Because I had been held in the ghetto during the war and lived an underground life using false documents after I left, I wasn't allowed to attend school. When the war ended, in just a few months, my uncle helped me with my education so much that I easily was able to enter a special high school, whose duration was only two years rather than the four years of the traditional model.

Student document.

During this period, I also was permitted to join the Scouts, an organization that had excluded Jews before the war. Thus, at fifteen years old, I had the pleasure of parading with the flag on national holidays, and I was proud to stand guard over the tomb of the unknown soldier.

As head scout with two monitors.

A dream come true.

My uncle Edmund's office was very sought after by Jews who wished to emigrate. He would provide documents that enabled people to exit via the Green Frontier between Poland and Czechoslovakia.

But when he was contacted by German natives (*folksdeutsch*), attempting their own rehabilitation with the communist authorities, he always adamantly refused them any type of assistance, despite being offered large sums of money for such work.

The *folksdeutch* were German descendants who had been born in other countries, such as Austria, Czechoslovakia, and Poland, but who considered themselves Germanic—one example was Hitler himself, who was Austrian—and insisted on calling themselves German.

In 1946, my uncle made the decision to emigrate to Australia, using papers sent to him by some Jews whose lives he had saved. Alas, it wasn't possible to achieve his goal.

At that time, the Polish underground army (AK) were systematically and brutally killing survivors of the Jewish intelligentsia; they would boast, "What Hitler couldn't finish, we will." And that's exactly what they did with my uncle.

After the war, at fifteen years old, a few weeks before leaving Poland.

My stepfather before leaving Poland.

My uncle Edmund—who had miraculously escaped Hitler's hell and risked his own life to save so many people by hiding them in the bunker—was shot and killed in cold blood, while leaving his girlfriend at her home after going with her to the movies. His funeral was attended by all those he had saved, as well as his attorney colleagues.

Mother in mourning for her assassinated brother in 1946.

The following is a translation of the funeral announcement:

Miraculously saved from the Hitlerite hell. Felled by an assassin's bullet in Katowice, July 6, 1946. Our best friend, great colleague, and unforgettable blessed memory,
Edmund Blum
Attorney
With great pain we feel the loss of this exceptional and honorable man, whose mission was to help his fellow man. Blessed is his memory.
Katowice, July 15, 1946.

Signed:
His circle of friends.

My mother put an announcement in the newspapers, offering a reward for whoever discovered the name of the killer, who had left a cap at the scene of the crime. The police carried out searches using dogs and the cap. Unfortunately, all of these efforts came to nothing, and the person responsible for his death was never identified.

In visiting our house to offer his condolences, the dean of the court and other colleagues advised us to leave Poland as soon as possible, to avoid another probable attack.

As a reward for their solidarity, Mother presented them with my uncle's stamp collection, which included many rare stamps.

Our Exit from Poland

Finally, we managed to obtain passports to leave Poland— but no exit visas. One dark, wet night, we left in secret for the railway station, bound for Prague.

After a week in Prague, we left for Paris. We stayed in Paris for six months in a guesthouse, and we were fed by JOINT (Jewish International Organization), a nonprofit entity set up to help Jews in difficulty all around the world.

We had decided to go to Brazil to meet Mother's sole surviving brother, Filip, who had been lucky enough to leave Poland before the war, in order to get to know this tropical country, which fascinated him.

When the war broke out, he tried every means possible to return to Poland to join the family but was unsuccessful. So he stayed in Brazil, tortured by the never-ending stream of tragic news.

Our problem was in obtaining entry visas. The Brazilian consulate, under the government of President Getúlio Vargas, systematically denied entry visas for Jews[12].

After some weeks, Mother, once again, came up with a solution to the problem. She returned to the consulate, taking with her the documents that proved our conversion to Catholicism. It did the trick, landing us the much sought after visas. Around six months later we embarked third class on the ship *Formose* destined for The Port of Santos, where we dropped anchor in 1947.

---

12   Recent studies reveal that the Brazilian government, influenced by racial theories coming from Europe at the time, was discussing whether it wanted the Jewish component in the Brazilian racial mix.

On the ship that brought us to Brazil.

During the trip, which took over a month, my stepfather got to know a chocolate technician who had worked in Poland for the famous chocolate manufacturer Wedel.

They decided to open a chocolate factory when they arrived in São Paulo.

Portuguese, Ora, Pois

Before we departed for Brazil, Mother enrolled us at the Berlitz Institute in Paris so that we could learn a little of the language of the land that had taken us under its wing. But there was a small detail that escaped our notice—the Portuguese taught there was from Portugal, not Brazil.

In a short time, we would say that we were going to "tumar" a coffee and "tucar" the doorbell. We would politely say, "faiz favoire," "até a bista" and "dá-me lischencha"—pronunciations that would make no sense in Brazilian Portuguese.

When we finally arrived in Brazil, we quickly wanted to put the language we had learned to use, but the first time Uncle Filip heard "faiz favoire[13]," he begged us, "Forget everything you've learned. They don't speak like that here."

---

13   "Excuse me", or "Do me a favor".

Arrival in Our
"Promised Land"

When we arrived, Uncle Filip and his great friend Motel Bergman were waiting for us at the port. He gave each of us a warm hug, hardly believing the miracle of actually being able to see us again. We went to his house in São Paulo, where he lived with his wife, Herta, his stepdaughter, Bárbara, and their daughter, Miriam. We stayed with them for three months, the time we needed to find a house of our own to rent.

As soon as we had settled into our new home, my stepfather and his business partner opened a small chocolate factory in the garage of the house.

The production, despite its high quality, didn't work out. The climate in Brazil, and the lack of technical knowledge about preservatives, meant that mold attacked the kilos of chocolates,so they had to be discarded.

In 1948, a year after our arrival in Brazil, my stepfather passed away, at the age of fifty-four. He was the victim of a brain hemorrhage caused by several aggressive blows he had suffered to his head during the war.

His death meant I had to interrupt the correspondence course I was taking at Mackenzie University. So I began to work as a manager in the fashion stores Monaliza and City, owned by Mr. Tabak.

But it wasn't all sad news. At a party, I met the first and only real love of my life, my future husband, Mauricio A. Braun. He was a civil engineering student in his last year at Politécnica at University of São Paulo.

Both wise and dedicated, he became a safe port for

me, where I could anchor the wreckage of a ship that had been hit by the immeasurable losses of loved ones and of my own identity.

During our engagement.

My husband, Mauricio.

Already a civil engineer, following our wedding he also graduated at Bachelor of Law, was recommended by the Appeals Court Ministry for the position of police technician in São Paulo, was elected president of the Brazilian Institute of Forensic Investigation–(IBAP), and was a teacher at the Police Academy of São Paulo.

My dear "sister"

Kora and Olek came to Brazil six months after we arrived, and we all ended up living together in the house we had rented.

She and her husband were not successful in finding work in the country, so after a while, they decided to leave for Buenos Aires. Saginur and Mundek Kramnitzer, a couple with whom they became friendly while in the ghetto, had already set up residence there.

Gicia and Max Saginur with their son, Jorge,
and Kora with her daughter, Rita.

In Argentina they found the happiness they were looking for. Not only did they find work, but they also welcomed Rita into the world, the daughter I mentioned previously.

Right up to the end, Kora played sports on her vacations in Villa Gesel and went fishing with friends at night, wrapped in newspapers beneath her sweaters to protect her from the cold.

Unfortunately she died of cancer in 1986, the disease that also killed my uncle Filip and my mother, who, until the year before her death, was as lively as ever, busying herself preparing all her old tasty tidbits in the kitchen. It was no coincidence that all three of them were smokers.

Shared Destinies

The couple Max and Gicia Saginur had a son called Jorge. During the war, Max and Gicia had hidden with their friend, Mundek Kramnitzer, in a bunker built by Staszek Jackovski, a great friend of Max's.

Gicia had been pregnant previously, in the bunker, but had sadly lost the baby and suffered complications after the birth. Her placenta was not fully expelled from her body, and she ran the risk of dying from an infection. The women present pressed down on her abdomen to try to induce the release of the placenta, but they were unsuccessful. Someone with small hands needed to reach inside her uterus and remove the residue.

So it was that dentist Mundek Kramnitzer intervened to save Gicia's life.

Having survived so much misfortune together, the Saginur couple and their friend Mundek remained inseparable for as long as they lived.

From left to right: Gicia, Mundek, Kora, Olek, and I. In Paris while waiting for visas for South America.

Two couples. From left: Kora, Olek, Gicia, and Max.

A New Life

My marriage to Mauricio was celebrated at the Beth-El temple by Rabbi F. Pinkus, and to my immense joy, Mauricio took to Mother like she were his mother too.

One year later, this happiness reached new heights with the birth of Eliana, the best daughter one could ever wish for. She is also a great companion, an exemplary mother, an attentive friend, and a talented speaker and writer.

Our wedding in 1951.

Watching her blossom in the land that welcomed my family without asking who we were or what faith we adhered to when we arrived was particularly gratifying for me.

Two years later, we were blessed with another gift— the birth of our son, Edmundo, who inherited my father's sense of humor and the same talent for imitations. He also has been my tireless advisor and a master of information technology, and even photography.

Our son, Edmundo, in the center.

Professionally, my children have followed the same, very successful, path as their father.

Eliana graduated from University of São Paulo in occupational therapy and began a successful career as a criminal forensic scientist for the Criminal Institute, specializing in ballistics and document analysis.

Edmundo graduated in law and also became a criminal forensic scientist for the Criminal Institute, specializing in document analysis and special forensics, as well as being a teacher at the police academy in São Paulo.

Our children, Eliana and Edmundo.

The four generations. From right to left:
Mother, me, Eliana, and Claudinha.

Another great source of pride is our three marvelous
grandchildren, to whom we have been very close since
their births.

Eliana presented us with Claudia, a lawyer graduated
from Pontifical Catholic University of São Paulo, and with
Eduardo, an engineering graduate of Politécnica at University
of São Paulo. Claudia and Eduardo have almost everything in
common—the same courage to tread new paths; the same
determination to advance professionally; the same desire
to grow intellectually; the same enthusiasm for physical
exercise; and the same enormous affection for us.

The last hug between Mother and "Claudinha" in Guarujá.

Colleagues at Politécnica: Mauricio and my grandson, Eduardo; shortly after being accepted for the renowned school in 1997.

Eliana with my grandchildren Claudia and Eduardo.

My daughter-in-law, Lilian, my youngest
grandchild, Allan, and Edmundo.

Edmundo and his wife, Lilian (my daughter-in-law
and friend, who is of like mind with me on many things),
presented us with Allan, our youngest grandchild, who
graduated from Pontifical Catholic University of São Paulo
in Digital Media and Technology. He is easygoing and
loving, and he knows exactly what he wants and goes
after it. I have never seen anyone with as much knowledge
on computing, nor anyone as willing to help me solve my
problems with computers (which are numerous), even by
telephone.

My husband, now retired, dedicates his time to writing
a book and creating different objects from metal, such as
chess pieces.

And this is my small family, the main reason for
my happiness. I admire and love each one of them
unconditionally. I live for them, making every effort not
to intrude on their decisions. I always say that when my
children were very young, Mauricio and I conducted the
orchestra, but nowadays we have moved into the audience.
We are the type that enjoys applauding.

Mauricio and the chessboard and pieces he made.

New and Old Friendships

Happily, I can say that I get on well with people. Hence I made new friends when my children studied at the Jewish school I. L. Peretz. I was a member of Muterat, the mothers' committee at the school.

I also have made friends through the Associação Brasil Parkinson (the Brazilian Parkinson's Association), for which I have been a volunteer and supporter for ten years. This association was founded by Marilandes and Samuel Grossman, and it offers free consultation in the areas of speech therapy, physiotherapy, psychology, and nutrition, as well as activities such as art workshops, a choir, a chess club, and others.

I also maintain the friendships that began on my arrival in Brazil in 1947, such as those with my precious Polish friends, who are also survivors of the Holocaust. In alphabetical order they are Ala Gartner, Janina Decol, Lila Knobloch, Marysia Angielczyk, and Raquel Gotthilf.

Mauricio and I were involved in founding the Bertie Levi store from B'nai B'rith and were twice presidents of this charitable and cultural association, through which we made friends so dear that we consider them family.

As this book is also dedicated to the search for a better world, I feel I have to write about some of the activities of B'nai B'rith, whose three-pillar mantra is charity, brotherhood, and harmony.

Its work, particularly in human rights and philanthropy, is tireless. One of the most beautiful examples of its contribution is the work it carries out with needy children inside and outside the community, such as in the Campaign to promote Visual Acuity. In this program, children who have problems with their sight are medically treated via visits to shantytowns and high schools on the outskirts of the city. They receive follow-up medical consultations and contact lenses—all for free. There have even been cases where tumors were detected and successful surgical procedures have been performed.

But as for people who are part of my life, I have been blessed with nephews and nieces from Mauricio's side of the family as well as one very special friend, my sister in-law, Paula Braun.

Fortunately, there are many nephews and nieces and great-nephews and nieces. Forgive me if I don't mention their names, but they all know that they live in my heart.

On my side, in Brazil I have just the one cousin, Miriam Blum Nudelman, daughter of my uncle Filip Blum and wife of Jacob, with whom she had a daughter, Patrícia, and grandchildren, Felipe and Jasmim.

My sister-in-law, Paula Braun, and me.

Uncle Munio with Mother in Cannes, France, in the seventies.

In Buenos Aires, there is Rita—daughter of my sister, Kora—married to Norberto Sandkovsky, and their children, Uriel, Ariel, and Martin. Also living there are my cousin, Gregory Hitner, his wife, Cecilia, and their children; and Jorge and Vivian Saginur and their children, Tamara and Alan, who are not family by blood, but are more than family in my heart.

In Israel, there is Sylvia Seibald, daughter of my dear "uncle" Munio Seibald, with her children, Roseli and Miron, and her grandchildren. Also in Israel is Frida, a friend miraculously spared from the Holocaust, and one so dear to me that I consider her family. She is married to Moshe Katz.

If I have forgotten someone's name, I ask him or her to forgive me.

A recent picture, taken at Mogi das Cruzes University,
where I gave a lecture and this exposition of my
photos and documents was displayed.

Interviewed by Marília Gabriela, for Brazilian television.

During a lecture given at the Congregação Israelita Paulista (CIP).

A Warning to Future Generations

For many years now, I have been dedicated to visiting schools and universities, and to making some TV appearances, to talk about the Holocaust, which to my absolute perplexity and indignation is still denied at times or, at best, is something people have never heard of. I am a survivor of everything that is recorded in these pages, and I witnessed what happened with my own eyes.

I consider it my mission to share what I saw. It's a commitment that I made to myself in an attempt to ensure that future generations are not taken by surprise and attacked in the manner we were.

Tragically, history could repeat itself and target any minority. Be alert. Be ready to respond immediately to any kind of physical or verbal aggression, however small it may be. It isn't difficult to damp down a spark, but a spark needs only a gust of wind to turn it into an uncontrollable blaze.

The world is sick and has not learned from the extermination of over six million Jews, homosexuals, Jehovah's Witnesses, gypsies, and mentally ill people—individuals whose only crime was to have a different faith, race, origin, or sexual orientation.

To the Nazis, a living Jew had the same value as an insect. And when dead, they were exploited wholesale as goods or trophies. Their hair was used to make pillows for the soldiers. Their skin was made into lampshades. Gold crowns and fillings were melted down and sent to Germany in bars. From body fat they made soap, which was sold in street markets and carried an unbearable odor. Their bones were crushed and used for fertilizer. Even the skulls were taken—to Germany, as souvenirs—to be displayed on the desks of their executioners.

It is important to point out that the victims of Hitler and his followers weren't even allowed the right to graves and headstones. Having been tortured, some were thrown into mass graves, while others were gassed using Zyklon B and then incinerated, transformed into black smoke that dissipated up the chimneys.

I have decided to leave for posterity this written record of the terrible and real events that I lived through, of which I was a victim, because words are blown away in the wind and time erases memories. But the written word remains.

It is my belief that the much sought after and longed for "peace on earth" will become possible only when human beings learn to exercise unconditional solidarity, tolerance, and respect for their fellow humans.

Remember, always. Forget, never!

Rita Braun
Born Henrieta Roza Hitner

Voyage of No Return ...

The sealed wagons
Carried human beings
Or only names
To places strange.

They all went together,
Men, women, and children,
In their faces fear and suffering,
In their eyes a thread of hope.

Black smoke filled
The cold and distant sky.
Not a tear was shed
Under the bright stars.

Not a grain of earth was thrown
Onto the giant grave,
The only welcome, Silence,
In those fields of green.

Rita Braun

In 2001, a visit to the cemetery beside the
Terezin concentration camp.

Tombstone in memory of the Jews from the city of
Katowice who succumbed during the Holocaust.

In memory of victory.
For the Jewish community of Katowice that was annihilated at the
hands of the German invaders, in the years between 1939 and 1945.
This spot was the location of the Great Synagogue, which was
destroyed by the Nazis in Elul 5699 (September 1939).

Yizkor for Six Million

We who survived the extermination,
Who were lucky enough to be born after the Holocaust,
Will honor the memory of those who,
with a gun in their hands
And panic in their hearts, died heroically,
Fighting while knowing that victory
would not be part of their story,
Succumbing in the ruins of the burning ghettos,
Dying of thirst and burning with fever.

Massacred, tortured, exhausted.

In the camps they were stripped of
everything, of even the right to a grave.
They were burned, reduced to ashes,
so that nothing remained.
With terror in their eyes and muted cries on their lips,
In the frozen wastelands, they were torn away
from fathers, pregnant mothers, and children.
The fat from their bodies was turned into soap,
Their skin made into lampshades, their
hair stuffed into mattresses,
And their skulls were left to adorn
the desks of their murderers.

To our people so cruelly exterminated at

Auschwitz, Majdanek, Treblinka,
Sobibor, Janow, and the ghettos,

WE PROMISE NEVER TO FORGET.

Rita Braun
Holocaust Survivor
Of the Stanislavov Ghetto, Poland